No (**Business**
The   **ıess Owners to**
Autc   **ble Your Sales**

ISBN: 9781068750403 Paperback

Published by: Inspired By Publishing

The strategies in this book are presented primarily for enjoyment and educational purposes. Every effort has been made to trace copyright holders and obtain their permission for the use of copyright material.

The information and resources provided in this book are based upon the authors' personal experiences. Any outcome, income statements or other results, are based on the authors' experiences and there is no guarantee that your experience will be the same. There is an inherent risk in any business enterprise or activity and there is no guarantee that you will have similar results as the author as a result of reading this book.

The author reserves the right to make changes and assumes no responsibility or liability whatsoever on behalf of any purchaser or reader of these materials.

Foreword

When Chris told me that this book was going to be called *No One Gives A Sh*t About Your Business*, I laughed. Of course I did, because it's funny right?

Not only is it funny because of the swears (and I'm always here for profanity), but it's exactly the kind of title I would expect from Chris. He has a knack for bringing people in, making them feel super safe whilst remaining the cheeky chappie he is, and then blowing everyone away with his genius.

The first time we met, Chris asked me if I liked chicken. I replied, "I love chicken!" He then offered me the crook of his arm and told me to take a wing.

I, of course, was sold, and we have been linking arms ever since.

Chris has helped me grow my warm leads list by the thousands, contributing to the revenue generation within my business to – at the time I write this – over £1.3 million.

What I love about Chris and his work is that his knowledge and genuine care for the customer are front and centre of everything he does. He actually *does* give a shit about people's businesses. I love the irony of the title of this book, as it is authored by a man whom I know cares deeply. If there are shits to be given, Chris is your guy.

What he has to share about the concept of customer journey and the necessity for automation, is not only super valuable, but does exactly what we all need to be doing right now more than ever: remembering that our leads are *people*. Actual real people, with busy lives and problems that need solving. So many business owners lose sight of this very simple fact and, as a result, find themselves scratching their heads when their marketing doesn't convert to sales.

I implore you to take this book, read it again and again, and implement what you need, even if it's only a bit at a time–you will not regret it.

Go get 'em.

Dani Wallace
CEO IATQB Ltd
Founder The Big Festoon
www.iatqb.com
www.thebigfestoon.co.uk

Contents

Introduction

When it comes to most businesses, their owners more often than not have two wishes: They want more sales, and they would kill for more time in the day.

Whilst this book can't give you more hours per day, the principles and learnings in each Chapter will allow you to convert more leads into sales, and give you time back that would otherwise have been spent on tasks that aren't bringing in money.

By the end, you will have a different perspective on how your prospects think, the importance of their customer journey and experience, how automation can revolutionise both that experience and your time, and how to pull it all together to improve your business.

The problem stems from the fact that, very often, people focus on marketing and sales. But they forget there is a step in between. Your campaigns *may* generate leads. Your salespeople *may* speak to your audience and get them to buy.

But the customer experience is almost always overlooked by smaller businesses. What happens from the point where they enquire to the point where they hand over their money is vitally important, and the quality of that journey isn't discussed or focused on anywhere near as much as it should be.

Simply put, the better experience your prospects have, the more likely they are to buy from you.

We all have that restaurant we go to because the service is brilliant, even if the food isn't the best in town. We all remember an interaction with a business in the past where the stand-out part was the experience with a staff member. This isn't a concept that many disagree with; however, this book will alter your perspective on what that initial customer experience looks like to get the most out of it for everyone.

You'll read this sentence a lot: Your prospects do not give a shit about you and your business.

This book will challenge you to see the planning of that customer experience from the perspective of someone interacting with your business, who, frankly, doesn't give a shit about you yet.

They don't. Why would they? Who are you to them?

All they care about is whether you have a solution to a problem they have, or if you can truly deliver such a pleasurable experience, that it is worth parting with their hard-earned money.

If you look at the customer journey from your perspective as a business person, you might be misaligned with your customer's mindset. After all, you care deeply about your business, having committed your time and effort to it. But your customers may not share that same level of commitment, and that could have a devastating impact on your bottom line.

Remember, you will never know the sales you are missing out on by not doing things.

You see this all the time: 1,000 people might land on a landing page, but only 10 fill out a form. You will never know why the other 990 didn't complete it, you will just assume that "They must not be interested." And that is a damaging assumption to make. After all, they were interested enough to click on the link that got them there in the first place, right?

Businesses have a habit of just accepting that the majority of people going through a process will drop off. Why does it have to be a matter of just accepting that and doing it all over again? If a campaign that generated 100 leads only creates 5 sales, most businesses will just repeat the campaign to get another 5. I would argue that you have 95 people there who just need a better experience.

Often people will talk about the fortune in the follow-up, and the importance of following up with prospects. That is featured in this book, and it *is* important. But I would go a step further: The fortune is in making your prospects feel cared about.

As you progress through the book, you will see not only the importance of having automation in your customer journey, but also the necessity for it from both a business perspective *and* from a customer experience one. Automation isn't trying to replace the human; it is making sure the customer interactions with your business are enjoyable, helpful and progressive.

Years ago, I spoke to a business owner who enlisted my services to generate leads for his business through paid social media ads. The product was a minimum £500 investment, and aimed at parents with children (mainly girls) aged 3 to 12 years old. As it wasn't an impulse-buy type product at that level of investment, plus it was always a bespoke order, we ran adverts that were lead generation forms.

To ensure quality, we listed the starting price of £500 in the adverts, and echoed that throughout the form they were completing. This way, we knew everyone was aware of the price before enquiring. We also asked two custom questions, as well as the standard personal information, to make sure they were thinking about what they were doing.

The campaign launched on a Friday, and over the first weekend generated 250 leads at a cost of roughly £1.06 per lead. I'll be frank, I started writing the case study at that point. It was, on paper, one of the most successful campaigns we had launched at that stage. I knew the client would be over the moon! We booked a meeting for Wednesday that week, and I went into it excited. One of the first questions I asked was "How many of them have bought so far?"

And I was bewildered to receive this response: "I haven't called any of them yet."

Until that point, I had assumed every business would have a follow-up process laid out for their business. The notion that people see an ad for a few seconds, fill out a form in under 40 seconds, and are then expected to reach out to this business and immediately give them money blew my mind.

That particular business's strategy was to email all of the leads that came in during the week on a Friday, BCCing them all, with no other follow up. This approach almost always results in the emails going to spam. And yes, that does mean if you enquired with their business on a Saturday, you would be waiting six days for one solitary email.

By the end of the campaign, it had generated 1,200 leads at just over £1 a lead…but only two sales. Coincidentally, those two sales came from people who filled out the form on a Friday.

This isn't uncommon in the business world. Marketeers will run campaigns aimed at getting leads, and will call them a success when they do. That campaign, through all "marketing" metrics, was a success. It did what it was meant to do: attract leads.

The problem is, leads mean nothing. Sales do. Leads don't pay the bills, customers do.

Leads are incredibly important, and in this book you will explore ways to get those leads in. But if their experience isn't good after that enquiry stage, you might as well take that money and throw it out of the window. At least that way, you might get some goodwill from a random social media post.

The other issue is, your sales team will attempt to call all of those leads. When these leads don't respond, they will say one of the complaints a sales team constantly says: "These leads are poor."

That friction between the sales and marketing sides of a business is commonplace in the entrepreneurial world. Yet everyone forgets what joins those bits together: the customer experience.

If you enquire with a business, and they take days to get back to you with nothing being sent to you in the meantime, are you more or less likely to buy from them? Most people say they are less likely, but hardly anyone would say they are more likely to spend money. And trust me, you want your prospects to feel more inclined to give you money.

By realigning your thinking on the prospect journey – as laid out in the first few Chapters of this book – and implementing the strategies, techniques and learnings from the rest of the book, you will be giving yourself and your business the highest chance of converting more leads into sales.

You will also notice that continuation of a quality customer experience will lead to more referrals, reviews and repeat customers, because people are inclined to revert to the businesses they have had a great experience with.

Finally, the biggest benefit I have found by reframing that thinking and implementing automation, is the time you get back. Time is by far the most important resource you have, and spending more of it stressing that leads aren't converting, whilst doing tasks that aren't working in general, is not the way time should be spent. That time you get back can be used for working *on* the business and *not* in the weeds of the day-to-day. As well, you can spend it with those you love.

My core purpose is to bring "Mickey Boat Moments" to other businesses. These are moments where you will feel what I felt when I finally got to tell my young son that we were going on a Disney cruise, or as he calls it, Mickey's Boat. I had the freedom of money to book the holiday, and the freedom of time to just block it out in the calendar.

That feeling of joy I got when he told me how excited he was, and when he constantly asked questions like "When are we going?" and "Can we watch Mickey's Boat videos?", that feeling is something better than almost anything I have felt before.

I want you to have those feelings. Those rare moments where you have achieved what you wanted to. The joy that can bring to others is immense.

I truly believe this book has the tools to build an expectation-exceeding experience between you and your customers, and will form the foundations for your business to grow and scale.

But first, you need to understand that no one gives a shit about your business.

During the book, you will have the opportunity to access a few exclusive free resources based on the Chapter you are reading. To interact as you are going along, scan the QR code below and I will WhatsApp you immediately. Then during the book, you can reply with certain words and receive the resources straight to your WhatsApp inbox.

Chapter 1
No One Gives a Sh*t

There are two things most business owners have in common: They all want more people buying their product/service, and they all want more time to be able to enjoy the fruits of their successful business.

If you have ever been frustrated by prospects ghosting you, not turning up to meetings and sales calls, or disappearing off the face of the earth after they have told you they want to buy, this book will help.

If you have ever struggled juggling the time allocated to following up prospects manually, been bogged down in the little tasks your business has to do and felt like you can't escape the day-to-day running of everything, this is for you.

Over the next 15 Chapters, you will learn that by understanding your prospect's mindset, behaviour and habits, combined with the ability to plan, automate and improve their experience with your business, you will be able to increase your conversion rates. You will also be able to give yourself and your team valuable time back to work *on* the business, not *in* the business.

The best bit is that this doesn't mean drastic changes to the business strategy, just a realignment of how you approach the customer experience. This Chapter is going to show how your prospects don't give a shit about you, and why understanding that is a good thing.

This fundamental understanding and shift in perspective will be the bedrock idea behind what you put in place for your prospects to experience. Because ultimately if you design what you do for people that don't care about the business, the ones that do care a little will be blown away.

As business owners, we are in the minority. According to estimates published by the Department for Business, Energy & Industrial Strategy, there were 5.5 million businesses in the UK at the start of 2022, of which 4.1 million were independent businesses with no employees. 99.2% of all businesses in the UK were considered small businesses, with less than 50 employees. Only 0.7% had between 50-249 employees and a minuscule 0.1% had over 250+ employees.[1]

Put simply, around 94% of the population aren't business owners. On top of that, every business owner is spread across different industries.

You don't get that way by being the same as everyone around you.

That is an amazing thing, but also it poses a problem. By nature, we think differently from most people we are appealing to. After all, if they thought the same as you did, they would have started a business themselves.

So it's important to emphasise this point: *No one gives a shit about your business.* No one should care more than you do in the first place, as that would be weird. If there is someone out there who cares more about your business than you do, that's a problem you probably need to address sooner rather than later.

For example, you have undoubtedly had a customer ask a question that you felt they should have known already, or that would be "common sense" in your eyes. Those questions are because your prospects do not care enough about you to have looked up the answers, or be experienced enough to know those answers first-hand.

I remember speaking to a prospect about their business and speaking in depth about the quality of the journey their customers were going through. The prospect just didn't care about what they experienced; he was so convinced that his product was that good, that people who needed it would buy it from him. "Why wouldn't they?" was always the answer. I said to him, "How regularly do you go to the doctors for checkups?", to which he answered coyly but indicated that it was rarely. I followed that up with, "Do you think a doctor would say 'Why wouldn't they come for a checkup?'" The point I was making is that people are people, and they don't care about things the same way you do.

I care about plenty of things more than others: my family, my relationships, both professional and friendly, my little luxuries, following a traditionally poor football team and making sure I make an impact on the people around me. I know I don't share the same values and care about things the same as others around me. That fundamental understanding is core to this book.

Why is this relevant to you? Because everyone who ultimately spends money with your business is a human being. They have different drivers, different priorities, different reasons to care about what you offer.

Understanding your prospects' mindset when they interact with you is game-changing, and allows you to put systems and strategies in place that reflect what they are likely to do moving forward. If you know what they are likely to do, it makes the chances of getting them to buy from you much higher.

We think differently as business owners. If we approach your prospect's experience through your business from start to finish the same way we would think about it as the business owner, then we are automatically way off the mark for the majority of people around us.

Another problem is that we surround ourselves with those who will, by nature, be the most supportive people for us, so we naturally get a warped view of how amazing everything we are doing is.

If you've ever had one person give you harsh feedback, the chances are that person can help you grow what you are doing, despite it being hard to hear.

We see this as businesses when we have an initial launch, and sales go well, with conversion rates as high as they can be and feedback is great! The problem is launches are usually done to communities that already know you; your friends and family. They are naturally more inclined to be more supportive and complimentary, however that can artificially increase your conversion rates, setting an expectation higher than reality.

Then, we launch it to a wider network through "colder" channels, like social media and to a market that hasn't heard of us before, and all of a sudden, the campaign performs a lot worse than we expected.

Granted, having a strong support network around you is something that is incredibly important, in my opinion. I've worked hard to network and surround myself with inspiring and incredibly supportive people, a lot of whom are the reason I can write this book. It is essential to have that for your own mental health rather than anything else.

However, one disadvantage to having a strong support network is that they become so close to you, they don't want to give constructive feedback that could actually help. Another is that they become blinded to what your standard customer would need because as they get close to you, they start to understand what you offer and the pain you help solve. Your customer might not know something blindingly obvious to your community because they know and love you.

Once you approach what your customer goes through from the lens of "No one cares," you start to put things in place that help everyone.

Rory Sutherland talks a lot about making your business as accessible as possible. While guesting at the Modern Wisdom with Chris Williamson podcast, during an episode called Surprising Insights Into Human Psychology, he states, "The idea of designing your business for the disabled is actually good business policy because you will actually find yourself with a target audience far larger than the one you originally anticipated."[2] And he goes on to state that the idea of making things more accessible will benefit more people.

If you put ramps around the building you own, everyone will find it easier to get into the building. If you make door handles easy to use for people with a lack of hand control, you will also be helping people carrying a cup of coffee when going through the same door.

You will *never* know what is going through the mind of every customer you have. Even if you asked every single paying client what they thought, which I will state would almost always be impossible, they would likely not tell you exactly the thoughts and emotions they were going through when they bought from you.

More importantly, you definitely won't know what is going through the minds of those who didn't buy from you, because most of the time you haven't got their contact details anyway. Those people are the ones that you are missing out on when it comes to revenue in the business.

A great example of this is the brand WD-40. If you don't know the story, it is quite an impressive example of determination. In the early 1950s, the company focused on creating a rust-preventing solvent to be used in the aeronautics industry and was actually used on the Atlas Missile launch. It is so named because they had 39 failed attempts to get the perfect product, and the 40th solution they came up with is still the formula they use today.[3]

That in itself is a story of persistence that we will cover later in this book, and one that shows how most businesses will give up earlier. But the part that relates to this Chapter specifically is that its original purpose was far from the mass-market appeal it has right now.

The senior management noticed a lot of the employees casually stealing cans of the product for use at home, and within a few years, they had engineered a way to get it into aerosol cans. Soon they rebranded to the name we all know and use today.

If they just ignored their staff sneaking the product out and didn't take the time to understand their mentality – which ultimately steered the company into the huge success it is today – who knows where they would be?

They did a good job of understanding how their clients thought and leaning into that.

No one gives a shit about the company and the branding realistically. It's a cool story, and at points an inspirational one, but no one really cares. They keep buying the products because they care about not having squeaky doors among other things. The reason you likely haven't heard of the story of WD-40 is because you don't care that much.

If the directors of the business thought that their customers care about the story of the company, that would be all you would see in their marketing. And in truth, the fact you haven't is a good thing. They know what people care about, and have grown since then.

But let's say, in a utopian world, every one of our potential customers loved what we do and did care about our businesses. That world unfortunately doesn't exist, but let's say it does. Most businesses still don't take into account the fact that people are inherently different.

Most personalities generally fall heavily into one of four categories: dominance, influence, steadiness and conscientiousness.

Simply put, even if everyone cared about you, the way one person interacts with your business will, by default, not be the same as the majority of people. Whilst these different personality profiles are not a four-way 25% split of the population by any means, it is safe to say that presenting what you do in the way that works best for you is not likely to be the best way for most of your customers.

The following is very much a generalisation, and I implore you to look deeper into personality profiles. But there is a theory that states that people who are more dominant in their profiles will act faster.

Those who are more steady will need a lot more time to make their decisions, as they don't like being rushed. Those who are influential are more optimistic in their approach, whilst those who are conscientious have a focus on quality and accuracy.

With that in mind, you need a process that can speed up in helping quick decision-makers without bombarding them with unnecessary information, while having that same information readily available to those who need it. It should also demonstrate success stories for those who are more optimistic and provide details and accuracy for those who need them. This obviously isn't an easy task.

One thing I want you to take away from this Chapter is that the way you think is very rarely the same way that most of your clients think.

Putting aside the fact they don't care about you, they will rarely be of the same mind, in general. And for clarity, I don't want you to put that fact to one side – it's in the name of the book.

But once you do, take that step back and look objectively at the processes that your clients, prospects and leads go through without being swayed by your own bias. You will start to design a more effective and higher-converting process that is more enjoyable for everyone.

Here Lies My Biggest Realisation

Once you get your head round the fact that no one cares, you start remembering all those times you have interacted with a business, and one tiny thing about the process made you give up.

You see, when people don't care about your business they give up really quickly.

Your website takes more than two seconds to load? Nope, I give up.

The information I am looking for is not in front of me when I click a link? Nope, too much effort.

Your payment process not accepting Apple/Google Pay, which means I have to get off the sofa to find my card? Nope, maybe next time.

And remember, you will never know that this has happened, because a business will never know why people didn't buy. They will make assumptions, and those assumptions are often wrong.

How does this help? Because you will never know why people who would benefit from what you offer aren't buying, the assumptions we make aren't always helpful. "They aren't buying because of the economy", "No one has any money", "Brexit is putting people off spending". It's all cliché, but it's also taking the blame away from you. Frankly, you're making excuses without looking internally.

Once you understand people simply don't care yet, with no malice intended, you will start to engineer everything within your business with them in mind. That customer focus will allow you to optimise their experience, and throughout the rest of this book we will explore what that looks like, including how doing it well will save you time and ultimately get more people buying.

It infuriates me to speak to marketers who look at a campaign and simply accept that X amount of people will register interest and Y amount of people will buy, without looking at the steps between those two points to work out what is putting them off.

We seem programmed to understand that a 1% conversion rate from a website is standard and that 99% of people visiting a site won't be interested. Yet if we do a good enough job of setting expectations at the start, aiming people towards a page that is relevant to what they are looking for, is easy to navigate, is enticing, functions the way it should, is fast, and has all the payment options needed, that number will increase.

Ask yourself this: How many times have you given up on a process that you would likely have given money to because of something small? How many times have you enquired with a business and not heard back from them, despite being ready with a budget? How many times have you registered your interest and been left without knowing what happens next, so you've not followed up?

Now ask yourself whether anyone going through your process will feel that or if they will feel nurtured all the way through.

You know more about your business than anyone else does. Or at least you should.

Your prospects will undoubtedly know less than you, which by deduction means they will have unanswered questions when going through the process. Remember, people will not buy from you if they are unsure about it.

If people aren't getting answers to their questions in the process of enquiring with you or looking at your products, they will simply give up. And you won't know; you don't get that feedback.

This often leads to mistakes from business owners, because their assumptions on what their prospects are thinking are rarely correct.

"No one is buying in the industry right now." Is that what they said when you asked all of them?

"No one can afford it right now." Did they show you their bank account?

"People need a discount to buy." Is everything you buy discounted?

Sometimes, elements of those assumptions will be correct, but I'd go as far as to say it is rarely the case that one is the sole reason people aren't buying.

Often the only reason they aren't buying is they have some doubts about the value exchange they are receiving. Their money for what you offer doesn't seem like a good deal to them because they don't have the information needed.

And at the core of it, they don't care enough to change their own minds.

In my opinion, it is one of the reasons that most local businesses that branch out fail.

If a local business has the support of the community, they often generate more loyal customers, returning customers and referrals. They have a story about "the local business that we are giving back to", which helps them get further in that process. And the loyalty of those customers often masks any downfalls in the process.

When they start expanding outside of the local area, they lose that and don't realise how big of a deal it is.

They overestimate how much people will care about the story because up until that stage, the only people they have been dealing with have been telling them how good it is and how much they love the story.

Your friends, family and support network are likely doing that to you at the moment. That is a good thing, as mentioned before, but it isn't the way the wider market will view you and the business. And that is something you need to understand.

Because you know more about the business, the best people to test what you are doing are those who know nothing.

They are the people who will tell you they didn't understand a certain point you made in your process. They are the ones who will tell you the process was a little slow, or they struggle to get answers to the questions they actually need to be answered, which is the difference between them buying and them giving up.

Because they don't care about you, they don't care about hurting your feelings, so they won't hold back telling you what is really not working for them.

A business can learn a lot more from negative reviews than positive ones. That isn't usually an uncommon assertion. We want to know what is going well and indeed need to know, but if the same complaint comes up again and again, it's something worth changing.

And where do negative reviews come from? The people who care the least about your business. If they actually cared they would have spoken to you, not left a review on social media for the world to see.

It is a good thing to realise that no one gives a shit, because when you do, you can design the process that will improve their experience and your bottom line.

In the following Chapters I am going to dive into why thinking your prospects do not care is the key to getting them to spend more with you. And the good thing is that when done well, it can give you more time back to work *on* the business, not *in* it.

Chapter 2
Your Leads Are People

Once you understand that people generally don't care about you, they just care about the solution you could potentially offer, you need to go back to basics.

This Chapter will go into detail on why understanding those prospects are actually human, with human problems, experiences and natural tendencies, is crucial to what is put in place within the business.

Many of the points in this Chapter will focus on businesses that rely on individual prospects that make some sort of enquiry before a sale is finalised, as well as the process a new enquiry goes through. I have found that this can work for e-commerce, but the processes are often a lot more condensed and "hands off", where businesses that need those leads coming through are likely to be more high-ticket, and more of a considered purchase.

Considered purchases are where people need to think for more than a small amount of time before buying, typically selling something that isn't regularly impulse-bought. This can sometimes be because the value of the purchase is higher, or the product / service itself is a big change to what they offer.

The main challenge with the more considered purchases is that the longer a sale takes, the more steps there are that people abandon the process, lessening the chances of them getting to the end.

If you're regularly frustrated or left thinking, "Why are they ignoring me, they were the ones that enquired!", then this is the Chapter where we start to dive into changing that.

Once you've understood that your prospects are human and that their being treated as people (not numbers) is the best way to understand what you need to put in place to generate more sales, you will see a huge difference in conversion rates from those leads.

That realignment of how you approach their experience will transform the expectations you are setting, the quality of the sales journey and the likelihood that those who don't care about you look past that and buy from you anyway.

There was a point in my life where I assumed this went without saying. But as I worked with more and more businesses, the notion that leads were more than just the numbers coming through a campaign actually seemed a rarity.

Now, I am not saying that businesses don't care about their prospects. You do. Frankly, you wouldn't be reading this book if you didn't care about them at all.

What I am saying is that it is easy to forget that the person on the other side of the marketing numbers has an actual life.

One of my most loathed sentences is "I get back to leads as soon as I can," which, on the surface, is a good thing. The issue is that it's all one-sided. It's when YOU can get back to them, but not when they necessarily wanted you to.

It also tends to lead to the assumption that if they don't pick up once or twice then they "clearly weren't interested" and "were a waste of time."

I hate that assumption.

If you've ever made an enquiry with a business, and they reached out at an inconvenient time, leading you to not pick up the phone, it doesn't mean you aren't interested, just that the timing wasn't right. Yet, that business will likely take your lack of response as a negative thing and eventually give up on you.

As business owners we rarely switch off from business, it isn't like a normal job that we can leave at the door when we step outside. This often means that you are responding to adverts or registering interest in things during non-working hours or outside of the norm. If you get a lot of your enquiries outside of the typical hours you would respond, that means you aren't alone in thinking that.

As such, a lot of enquiries to businesses are made at a time when no one would be available to reach out directly. They get the standard "thanks for your enquiry, we'll be in touch" email, which honestly doesn't happen all the time, but that often leaves them in limbo until a salesperson has the time on their day to reach out.

As such, that leads to the following: They try and reach out on a day that you have meetings stacked, or on a day where you are otherwise engaged, and tough shit. You aren't putting your life or business on hold to answer a call that you weren't ready for, even though you have registered your interest.

A gentle reminder here: *It is not your prospect's job to chase you to give you money.*

When was the last time you enquired with a business, didn't hear anything and that meant you called them and asked to give them money?

We will dive into making things easy in a later Chapter, but the very least you should do is not make it hard for someone who wants to give you money.

The reason you need to remember that your lead is an actual human being is that most salespeople make assumptions about why the call isn't being picked up, which is, laughably, rarely accurate.

Think about it for a second: How often do you make an enquiry with a business, and when they call you, the main reason you don't answer is because you aren't interested? You made the enquiry, you were interested at that point. And as long as it was made clear to you that there was going to be a call off the back of the enquiry, it's safe to say most people will want to have that conversation.

Too many businesses, and in particular marketers, that focus purely on leads and not sales, will look at a campaign and simply dismiss a large portion of their leads because they didn't pick up once or twice.

In my example above, my days are usually stacked. They book up quite far in advance, and typically, I struggle to take calls out of the blue. I need things scheduled in, and if you don't give me that facility, we will be playing our happy game of telephone tennis back and forth until one of us gets bored, and I guarantee it's more likely to be the business than the consumer.

Once you realise that the person on the other end of that unanswered phone is both a human with a life to lead and isn't waiting for your call with bated breath (because remember, they don't give a shit about you yet), you start to rethink what the process looks like.

First Impressions Matter

It might be a cliché but you have one chance to make a first impression. For physical businesses in a location, it is simple and standard to know that if the person greeting your client at the door isn't smiling, isn't in a good mood, lacks a professional appearance, and doesn't know what they are talking about, you are on the back foot.

As the age of the internet has grown, and in particular after COVID, that personal connection has fallen away somewhat. Somewhere along the line, we forgot that the time between the initial enquiry and that first point of contact is important.

If you went to a restaurant, walked through the door, waited at the sign that said "someone will see you soon, please wait here," and had no one contact you at all for five hours, it wouldn't be great service. (Side note: If you actually wait five hours in that situation, may I suggest you seek immediate medical attention?).

That may seem like an overly exaggerated example, but as a business, if you aren't consistently going back to your leads within a short space of time, they will just give up. Yet can you honestly say there aren't times when they are waiting hours, if not days for someone to go back to them?

They are humans, they have lives to live. And since they don't care about you yet they aren't anywhere near close enough to a sale to set aside time for a potential follow-up when "you are ready."

Throw into the mix that any enquiries made after, say, 8pm would likely be inappropriate to reach out manually to them until first thing the following morning. Which means, if you don't have something in place to nurture them in the meantime, they are going 12 hours without hearing anything from you. That is assuming you work the full weekend and an enquiry wasn't made on a Friday evening, which would then wait until Monday morning.

I don't know about you, but waiting 12 hours for a point of contact that impresses me isn't a great first impression. Yet most business owners would say, "But that is the first time I have to go back to them."

That is where you need to automate parts of the journey in a behaviourally natural way, something that will be a theme throughout this book, and something that, when done well will save you time and make the journey your leads will enjoy going through.

Let's take that restaurant example again. You've turned up at the restaurant, been seated at your table. Thirty minutes have passed since you ordered, and food hasn't arrived. For the most part, you'd be less than blown away by the situation.

Now, same scenario, but this time, you are greeted at the door with the server mentioning that the kitchen is a little backed up, and there might be a 35- to 40-minute wait for food. But they would do their best to get it out early. During that wait, they come over to update you on when the food is likely to come out. And when it does come out after 30 minutes, they say it was a little earlier than expected. But they value your patience. What then would be your impression?

It would be a safe bet to say that you would not only be happy, but would likely recommend the service to other people, and probably come up with a cliché line, "Worth the wait after all."

The only difference is, at the start, the server treated you like a human being and informed you of the wait, in case it would be an issue. They were covering the bases of if you had somewhere to be after dinner, making sure your expectations were set correctly. And in doing so, they left the decision to stay down to you.

As long as they then meet the expectations they set, you're all good to go.

There is a whole Chapter in this book on setting clear expectations, but the fundamentals behind that are that your leads are real human beings, and you need to treat them as such. In addition, they are humans that don't care about you yet, so what you put in place needs to be at a level that captures their interest, sets expectations and gives you a reason to stick around.

I feel this lack of human connection goes back longer than we think. We used to go into shops, take a number at the end of a queue, and get called up as a number. There wasn't much personal touch in that system until you spoke to someone, and the least enjoyable bit of it was waiting in the queue. That isn't a coincidence.

Fast forward to today's customer service lines for big companies that just keep you on hold, listening to some inevitably horrible music waiting to get round to you – that isn't fun. The ones that tell you, "You are number 4 in the queue" were an improvement. But when you have been number 4 for 25 minutes, it gets old really quickly.

You see, it's much easier to put tangible numbers against a budget for things when you look at data. Economists love this, but they don't take into account the fact that their data is comprised of actual human beings.

If you run a business where people attended your venue, having someone whose dedicated job was to make sure you were being looked after, and that your experience was as good as it could be, would of course have a positive impact on the human experience. But it is incredibly hard to say that

that person was covering their wage because there is no data to say that increase on experience was financially beneficial.

Yet, ask anyone coming back again and again, they would likely mention that person being at least a part of them returning.

In what seems like a previous life, I was a DJ in Mallorca for six years. My job was to entertain and keep people in the bar I was working in.

To set the scene, there were 15+ bars and clubs that for the most part were all free entry, had the same drinks, similar staff and similar music. Combine that with the fact that guests were only there for at most 10 to 14 days, and they were pre-programmed to want to see all of the different bars. You start to realise that the job of keeping people in the bar was actually quite a tough one. One wrong song would kill the entire bar, and that definitely happened.

What I learned to do better than most was look at the people, not the crowd. You learn as a DJ how to "read the crowd", but in most environments, the crowd wasn't prone to all leaving at the drop of a hat. You might lose a dance floor here and there, but you didn't lose the entire bar like you could in Mallorca.

I once lost 250 people within five minutes by playing that season's top song. This happened because one group from the University of Portsmouth's cricket team, along with a few other groups, were 40+ people who were on a night out with a game going. When that song came on, they immediately finished their drinks and left without context. Over 40 people walking the length of the bar to leave at the same time naturally brings a few more people that had finished or were at the end of their drinks with them. This means the crowd had dipped by nearly a third in one song, and that drop in atmosphere was noticeable. Within five minutes of them leaving, other groups had left, and the bar was practically empty.

I started learning how to focus on the people I had. And I ask this question a lot:

Imagine you were the DJ, in a bar with five stag parties and one hen party. The stags want typical stag music, singalongs, rock, indie, etc., while the hens want R&B and dance music. The bride-to-be herself wants pure cheese: think S-Club 7, Spice Girls, you know, the proper cheese. What do you play to keep the bar busy for as long as possible?

There is one correct answer, but most people don't get it right the first time. So if you did, perhaps a career in Mallorca as a DJ is on the horizon!

Most people would say you play either indie for the stags because there are more of them, and you have a better chance of keeping an atmosphere. Some say play for the hens with R&B, because if they stay then the guys might stay, which is partially true.

The correct answer is you play for one person: the bride-to-be. It's her hen party, so the hens are staying where she wants to stay regardless of whether they like it or not. If all of the hens stay, the stags will likely stay too. If you play R&B and the bride-to-be doesn't like it, the hens leave, albeit reluctantly. If you play for just the stags, the hens almost always leave, and the stags will eventually not want to be in a bar with just other stag parties.

I understood that human behaviours have layers, and all I had to do was work out how to get to the next step. "There are more stags, how do I keep them? I keep the hens. How do I keep the hens? I keep the bride-to-be happy. How do I keep her happy? Play her music, make her feel special, make a fuss of just her. Everything else falls into place after that."

People are creatures of habit, and whilst we are all different, there are behaviours that we tend to share for the most part. If you are running in a marathon, and the first 10 people go the wrong way, chances are the entire chasing pack will do the same. If you are walking down a street and everyone is running in the opposite direction, at the very least you aren't continuing down that street at the same pace you were before.

When we apply that to our businesses, we have to realise that one lead is not the same as another lead. They are different people.

For example, I hear the following sentence all the time: "Facebook leads aren't good." It generally refers to leads coming through Facebook lead forms. I hear cliches like, "People on Facebook don't spend money." Then I ask the person talking about it "Do you spend money on good products?", to which they usually say yes. Then, I ask, "Are you on Facebook?"

They always are.

We have so blindly listened to cliches and taken the human out of the process, that we believe leads from a certain place aren't good or they aren't potential clients and customers!

What is true more often than not is nothing to do with where they come from, but with the fact that their journey has been incredibly poor. Someone scrolling on Facebook as they are enjoying social media has seen your ad, which has interrupted what they were doing originally. Asking them at that stage to commit as much time and effort into going through a process as someone who has actively searched for what you do on Google, for example, is just being unrealistically optimistic.

That doesn't mean that the person who sees it on one platform is more or less qualified than another. It often just means they are at an earlier stage in the process. But because they are just "leads" we don't think about the person behind it.

Someone on Facebook would need more information sent to them to potentially get them to the point where they would want to Google it. But by that stage, they are bought into what you do and don't need to look elsewhere.

The issue with that?

Most businesses give up after trying to reach out to them once or twice, and don't do a good enough job of sending the information that would help after they have enquired.

And remember, they don't give a shit about your business. So if you have just grabbed their attention for the 15 seconds it takes to see a Facebook ad, complete a Facebook form and submit it, you asking them to be as qualified as someone actively searching for you is borderline laughable.

You need to grab their attention, keep it, and facilitate a persistent follow-up process that is built from a place of service, and gives them the ability to say it isn't for them, or indeed qualify them out on your side if you don't feel they are the right fit for you.

In later Chapters, I will cover how I facilitate this, and how regardless of where a lead comes from, by the time they get to me, they are excited, informed and have clear expectations of what it looks like to work together.

Chapter 3
Your Customers' Perspectives And Behaviours

As humans, we have traditionally haven't been great at understanding other people's perspectives. The history books will do a good job of showing what we, as a species, do when someone disagrees with us. It's not typically been a great outcome.

However, I would like to take this Chapter to separate from our history and our tendency to forget other people's perspectives and focus on exactly that.

Business owners are great at designing processes that are optimised to get someone to do the thing they want them to do, but they rarely look at it from the perspective of what they are likely to do. That may seem a little nuanced as a difference, but the hardest thing to do in sales is to go against someone's natural behaviour.

What do I mean by seeing things from their perspective? Simply put I mean that if you have a basic understanding of what someone's perspective is, you are more likely to plan out an experience that fits what they are familiar with.

For clarity, you won't be able to understand everyone's perspective in depth, and nor should you try. You will have a certain ideal customer, and most people will likely share the same set of problems that will drive them towards buying from you.

Understanding what led to those problems and what would be causing someone to consider investing in what you offer, will ultimately benefit you further down the line.

I get fed up with guru after guru telling you that to get someone to do something you have to use "persuasive" language and essentially trap them into a decision. People are smarter than that for the most part. And they know when they are being sold to, especially when it isn't being done with their best interests at heart.

We naturally gravitate to people who understand us. For example, most people would rather go back to the same doctor each time they need to because that doctor knows your personal history a lot more intimately than someone new.

Understanding what that person is likely to do means you can position the information you need to deliver in the best possible way for them. More importantly, when a prospect knows that you understand them, they will start edging closer to caring about you and the business. We can use this to lay the foundations for a healthy relationship between you and your prospect, which not only means they are more likely to buy, but they become advocates for your business.

You can only begin to understand what they are likely to do, and what is behaviourally natural when you start understanding they initially don't care about you, they are real people and they are likely to act in a certain way, a way that is behaviourally natural to them.

The point of this Chapter is you don't currently understand their perspective, and you need to have things in place to gather that understanding. Because what may seem natural behaviour to you isn't always the same as natural behaviour for them.

What is Natural Behaviour?

I talk a lot about behaviourally natural customer journeys, and how they are essential when it comes to thinking about and developing your own processes for prospects and clients.

It is important to remember what you read in the last Chapter, and how people are inherently different in their composition. When I refer to processes being behaviourally natural, it will never be absolutely perfect for everyone going through that process. Someone who acts incredibly fast will go through things differently than someone who requires a lot of questions to be answered.

What I want you to think about is what is the easiest thing for them to do next. Specifically, being very granular and detailed about those steps. One of the most difficult things in sales and marketing is to get someone to change a behaviour they already are used to.

People typically do one of three things behaviourally:

1. What they have always done
2. What feels natural for them to do, and
3. What they think everyone else is doing.

If you are trying to get them to do something new, that isn't like what they have done before, without evidence that other people are doing the same, it is an uphill battle from the start.

You should be making your process fit at least one of those three things.

I'll use the example of my own keynote talks from the stage.

Overall, my aim for the talks is to educate those in the crowd, increase interest and understanding of what I do, and of course increase my own community to help my business grow. Every time I do a keynote presentation, someone in the room will work with me in some capacity in the future.

If I focus on the community growing element, I have to break down what I want.

"I want people to give me their data to opt into my community." Knowing that, I could say at the end of my talks, "And if you want to be part of my world, come to the stand and give me your business card." That might work, but there is a more behaviourally natural way that can be achieved, and all I had to do was work backwards.

I want people to give me data. How do I do that quickly? QR codes are a great way of doing so since COVID, as everyone had to scan one to get into restaurants and venues. Most smartphones have a QR code reader in the camera automatically, so it's easy.

How do I get them to scan it? If I put the code at the end of the talk, it might seem like I am selling to them. If I put it at the start of the talk, they are more likely to do so.

How do I maximise people doing so? I say to them that for the next 40 minutes, I am going to make the talk interactive and if they don't scan it, they will be missing out. Plus, I will throw in a few freebies. Now I have tapped into their FOMO (fear of missing out), which is a powerful emotion.

What would stop people from scanning it now? Maybe their phone is in their bag, or in their pocket. That seemingly tiny objection at that stage I could dismiss by simply thinking "Well of course they will get their phones out, they would be lazy if they didn't," but that isn't a very good understanding of what is behaviourally natural.

So just before the slide with the QR code on it, I have a pattern interrupting slide that tells people to turn their phones from silent to loud, accompanied by my telling the audience that "I am going to do something other speakers will tell you not to do because I want to hear your phones going off during the talk." There is no objection to doing that; however they now all have their phones in their hands, so getting them to scan a QR code is a little bit easier.

All of those steps are thought out, and all the things I say on stage are deliberate at that point. They are all designed around what I have seen on stage when I have done the talk before, and I have understood what they are likely to do next.

As soon as they scan the QR code, they fill out a very simple form and they are sent a WhatsApp selfie of me with three options they can click, all of which are mildly self-deprecating. But importantly, they are incredibly easy things to interact with.

During the talk, I know that people will get their phones out again to take photos of the slides I have, and as soon as I do see that I tell everyone they can send me the word "slides" and it will send all of them in one go.

Now I have everyone sending me messages, everyone's phones loudly pinging in the crowd, anyone not doing it thinking "Everyone else is doing this, maybe I should too," and I am getting them from one mental state to another, in a behaviourally natural way.

All of this so that later in the talk, when I tell them to send me the word "meeting" to book a sales call with me, the steps are easy and similar to what they have already been doing.

To see the presentation follow up, send me the word **PRESENTATION** on WhatsApp.

For those who have scanned the code, you will have seen a few goodies that I have thrown in there too. And you will have noticed that it is an easy process to go through because I have thought about what would be the most natural thing for you to do at that stage.

And ultimately, you are now in my community regardless of where you got this book.

One of the greatest examples I have seen of misunderstanding what someone is likely to do was when I was driving on the M6 down to a conference.

If you haven't seen this before, occasionally in the fields dotted along most UK motorways, there are lorries parked with advertising on the side, aimed at the drivers. Inner cities have a lot of them around, but in the rural areas where motorways interject, they are often sporadically located in fields.

The idea of static billboards in town centres having QR codes is actually a smart way of delivering marketing. It's a clear call to action that requires them to scan the code and head straight to a website. People's curiosity often takes over and they will scan to see what they are missing, and the QR code can track exactly what billboard it came from. Overall, a smart campaign.

The issue I saw on that drive was someone had seen this idea and thought "I'm going to put that on the billboard next to the motorway."

At no point in that decision-making process did anyone stop to think that typically people driving 70mph down a road, storming past a static advert, are unlikely to get their phones out and try to scan a QR code – unless the ones who created the advert are banking on there being traffic, and the car passengers are bored enough to get their phones out. It is a beautiful example of not a single person thinking what the target audience is likely to do in that situation.

An equally mind-blowing example I have seen was on the way to Belfast, when I was stuck behind a party bus that was advertising all the services they offer, branded with all the party imagery that you would associate with a party bus. Stag dos, hen dos, 18th's, 21st's, proms, funerals, weekend getaways, birthdays, weddings.

Did any of those stand out to you?

I was the same. One of those was an interesting addition.

Now, I know that the company essentially offers transport for all occasions, and branching out in that situation is a good thing. However, if you needed cars for a funeral, I am guessing you are unlikely to go for the big party bus with disco balls painted on the side. Likewise, a party bus that specialises in the sombre atmosphere funerals are known for isn't a great selling point.

No one took a step back and thought about how people were likely to react upon seeing the multitude of different services.

I would hope that if someone was thinking about their customers' perspectives, they would come to the conclusion that leaving funerals out of the offering would be a sensible decision.

I think one of the difficulties is that we are so rarely our own customers. We may well have started our businesses as a result of a problem that we saw, but we don't always get to view our own processes as a customer.

More pertinently, if we did have a problem that our product/service solves, solving it doesn't usually involve going through our own processes – those processes are usually created after the problem is solved.

Take the example of childcare. When you are a first-time parent, finding what childcare you need isn't as simple as that may seem. You don't know what they would potentially be eligible for, you don't always know what year they start and how the allowances work in the region you are based. All you know is that you need the outcome.

If you are presented with the options without any context, you won't know what one to pick.

This happened with a client of mine when redesigning their inbound customer journey from scratch. It was timed incredibly well, as I was in the process of going through the application for childcare for my first child at that time. So I was experiencing all the unanswered questions.

They had designed the process initially to make it easy for people to choose the type of childcare they wanted. Full-time, part-time, wraparound school care, breakfast clubs. Lots of options, but I had no idea what the differences were and which one would be the best fit for my child.

They had the blind spot that they were trying to make it easy, but were forgetting the gap of knowledge a lot of first-time parents have, and skipped that bit.

As a result, they were spending a lot of time responding to questions that were being sent in that ultimately were the same question.

It may not seem like a lot of time being taken, but five minutes to respond to an email, to 100 different parents, a few different times a year, can turn into dozens of hours of work internally.

Moreover, the parents asking the questions were the ones who were most proactive in actually finding the email, writing their own email and sending it. That's quite a leap of effort at the early stages of an enquiry and not something people naturally do. So common sense suggests that more people who have the same issues simply haven't spoken up.

My rough rule of thumb is that if you have one person giving you feedback, there are 10x as many people who have the same issue but haven't voiced it out. There will always be people at your table in a restaurant who will answer the question "How was your food?" with "It was great," even if they hated every moment of it. Those people make up a much larger portion of people than those who will happily speak up.

With the childcare provider, once they understood that their customer's perspective was less informed than they had laid it out, they started putting sections in the customer journey that explained who would need to apply for what spaces.

The video messages they had that explained this not only informed the prospect of what they needed to do, but it also reduced the time that was spent answering questions to prospects internally (as the answers had already been given proactively), and it resulted in more people applying.

This was because a majority of prospects who didn't have the impetus to reach out off their own back were getting the answers to questions that would have held them back and prevented them from completing their application in the first place.

You will have experienced this when speaking with customers who have a higher level of experience than your normal customer. There is a point in the conversation when you realise the normal things you would have said at that stage would be stating the obvious and you adjust the information you are giving based on their level of expertise.

In person, this is easy.

In person, this is what you default to.

In reality, you have to treat every person going through your processes as someone who could know a large amount about what you do, and someone who has never heard of you before.

This is much easier said than done.

You should design the process to be accelerated for those that don't need the baby steps, but also clear enough that those who do need help receive the assistance they need.

The more accessible the process is, the easier it is for everyone. Those with experience can move on to the next step quickly, avoiding unnecessary hurdles. Meanwhile, those who need more guidance will find the necessary steps clear and straightforward."

One of the biggest things that helps with this while growing a business is finding people in your network who know nothing about what you do, and get them to go through the processes.

You should have around 5-10 people you send your processes to for testing; make sure you trust their opinion and ask them to give you the positives and negatives in equal value.

Ideally, these are people who likely wouldn't be your ideal customers anyway, because they will give you an outside perspective on the process that might be a complete blindspot for you.

They see things that you miss because you know what you do like the back of your hand. You naturally connect dots in your head better than your potential customer would because you know what you do better than they do. Those dots aren't always that obvious for brand-new prospects at the start of their journey.

Try at all times to think, "What would the prospect think at this exact stage?" or "What is the most natural thing for them to do when they don't care about me yet?" But you will always have blind spots in how you approach it.

By utilising a network of people, you can get valuable feedback that will help make your launch for the offering a little more effective. Just make sure you are clear with them that you are looking for things to improve, and that you won't take it personally if they give you good constructive feedback. You'd be surprised how quickly people will point out the bits they don't enjoy when they are sure they can't hurt your feelings, so be prepared!

For those businesses that don't have that network, you can do this with introductory offers for beta testers.

A great way to enact this is to do this for events or concepts you are offering for the first time. Limit the attendance to a small number, much less than the target will be when the final idea is launched. Offer a reduced rate in exchange for the understanding that they are part of a beta test, you are going to use them as "guinea pigs" and you will require their feedback as part of the offer. Set aside time after the event to speak to all of them directly, asking them three things they loved, and three things they would change.

Any themes that are consistent across the feedback, look at how you can improve the parts that could be improved, or keep the bits that are impressing clients.

That feedback takes time, but it allows you, as best you can, to see things from the client's perspective. That way, you cover as many of the blind spots as possible.

Now, there isn't a polite way of saying this: *Some of your prospects are idiots.*

There is also definitely a portion of the prospects you have coming into your processes that you don't want to work with. Understanding their perspective doesn't always mean you want to work with them and their point of view.

However, someone responding to you with the sentence, "I don't understand that" can be for a variety of reasons, and more often than not it is your fault they don't understand. Blaming them for not knowing something you are an expert in is frankly ridiculous.

An experienced driver doesn't look down on someone taking their first driving lesson with the attitude "What an idiot, how could they possibly not know that?" They have an understanding that you have to learn somehow and that takes time. Yet we don't apply that when comparing our prospect's inexperienced perspective against our own experienced business owner's perspective.

I cannot emphasise this enough: If someone who is willing to give you money and is a good fit working with you goes on to say, "I don't understand what you just said," that is your fault, not theirs.

If your customers are all used to paying by card for things in your industry, mandating they all pay on the invoice is going to cause issues, even if that is easier for you and saves you card-processing fees.

If your customers feel more natural using a mobile device to buy your products, designing a website to be desktop-optimised only is going to cause issues, even if that looks nice and is what you want them to do.

If you want them to fundamentally change what they naturally do, unless you have clear evidence of other people doing the same thing, they will feel they are out on their own and are unlikely to do it.

You'll get used to this reminder throughout this book: They don't give a shit about you enough to be the anomaly that sits outside of those three behaviours. Let's revisit them again. Your customers naturally do any one of these three things as they go through their journey:

1. What they have always done
2. What feels natural for them to do, and
3. What they think everyone else is doing.

You therefore need to ask yourself the question: Does what I am asking my prospects to do seem natural with one of those three behaviours?

Using Apple or Google Pay is commonplace nowadays, and is a hell of a lot more convenient. It has always been convenient since day 1, but it took a while to take off because it didn't fit in those three categories very well. It wasn't something they had always done (paying with their phones), it wasn't a natural thing for them (it wasn't similar to anything they had done), and at the start, people weren't seeing their friends and family doing it, so no one was doing it.

It took a strong, persistent, and frankly, pricey advertising campaign to push its value and essentially engineer the perception of the third behaviour. Now it is commonplace.

Studies predict that in 2026 over 60% of the global population will be using digital wallets[4]. Considering Google Pay and Apple Pay were only launched in 2011 and 2014 respectively, that is a massive leap.

Here's a hard truth. The chances are your product isn't going to take the world by storm to quite that extent. And you're also unlikely to have the kind of advertising budget Apple and Google have at their disposal.

You need to work less on changing their natural behaviours and lean into what is natural for them to do. Once they are your clients, you can work on changing certain behaviours.

Seeing things the way your customers see them, and guiding them in ways that are behaviourally natural is not only better for you, because of the quality of conversations you will have and the increase in conversion rates, but it feels nice for your customers.

If you are going through a process that answers your questions, feels logical, delivers information, makes it easy, smooth and has clarity throughout, you are going to be more likely to buy. So will your prospects.

The best way to begin understanding how your customers and prospects are likely to behave is fairly simple: Ask them.

Having feedback measures in place is incredibly important, as you need to be able to understand what drove them to you. Without that understanding, you are making assumptions, which can often be misaligned with what they are likely to be thinking.

This can be as simple as physically asking a selection of people directly for a period of time. Get on the phone, call the people who have bought from you and ask them what they liked, what they wanted, and what they think you can improve.

Failing that, having a step in your post-sale follow up process that asks for feedback and reviews when the feedback is positive, can be a simple addition that doesn't take as much time.

More in-depth processes can be market research sessions that bring people within your ideal target market and ask them beforehand. Viewers of BBC's *The Apprentice* will know that in a lot of the challenges, part of the process is putting their ideas to a consumer research panel that often gives them critical but valuable feedback. As a business, this can show you blind spots that you may have missed before.

Supermarkets have spent millions over the years working out what their customers are likely to do when entering their stores. In larger supermarkets, they will typically have a section at the front of the store that is homeware or fashion, that has large profit margins and is often higher priced.

This is rarely the reason someone would go to the shop, but that impulse addition to the basket can massively increase the average order value of customers.

The aisles that you navigate round the supermarket are also laid out very particularly, in a way that feels natural and attempts to make it easy for you to find what you are looking for. If you've ever felt frustrated at the supermarket moving things round, it is because you have a way of doing things that has been disrupted.

Even the placement of items on the shelves is strategic; those at eye level are the ones the supermarket wants you to buy, whether they have higher margins or are own-brand products. The lower priced items are typically on the bottom shelves, very deliberately.

Finally, they put the small, easy-to-grab items at the checkout counters, so you can simply grab them and add them to your shop/basket. It wouldn't be a great place for a TV to be positioned, but chewing gum or gift cards are easy additions at the last minute.

All of this has been done by conducting extensive studies and research into what their customers are likely to do. Whilst as a small business you can't be expected to do it, it's worth knowing that the millions being spent globally is for a very good reason.

In this Chapter, we have covered understanding that your prospects are likely to behave in certain ways, and trying to change what they would naturally do is a lot harder than understanding and leaning into what they are likely to do anyway.

Remember, people do one of three things; what they have always done, what feels natural for them to do and what they think everyone else is doing.

You have understood that viewing your customer experience from their perspective can often show you blind spots that you are missing as the business owner, which are ultimately holding you back.

And to help identify those blindspots, utilising the people around you to help give you constructive feedback in both a positive and a negative way.

Asking your audience is a great way to achieve this, as they are collectively going to be able to inform you what they are looking for better than you can.

Jimmy Carr, a comedian from the UK, talks about this when planning out jokes for his live shows. He talks about how the audience is a genius: You could plan out the best joke you've ever written, send it to your comedian friends and close circle and they all agree it is great. Then when you stand on stage and deliver it, if no one laughs, it isn't a good joke.

It doesn't matter how much everyone around you loves it; the audience will tell you if it is funny or not with their reactions because they are collectively the genius.

It is the reason why most comedians have smaller, more intimate shows that they can test-drive some material before it is shown to the wider world.

Russell Howard, another UK comedian, would have free-to-attend intimate shows for around 50 people the day before his live taping of *Russell Howard's Good News*, where a lot of the material is the same but anything that falls flat in the room of 50 doesn't make the final taping.

Once you have a clear understanding of your customers' likely behaviour and recognise that they don't care about you yet and have real problems, you can start optimising for what you need them to do.

Lean into what they are likely to do, using your foundational knowledge to guide your strategy. We do this, by making their journey as easy as possible.

Chapter 4
Do as Lionel Says: Make It Easy!

The great singer Lionel Richie said it best, "That's why I'm easy!" If you're anything like me, I apologise for that song being stuck in your head for the rest of the day, or at least the chorus!

Make It Easy for Them to Give You Money

This Chapter will focus on the importance of making things easy for your ideal prospect. What does that mean? It means thinking from the perspective of someone who doesn't know your business, and yet with limited knowledge will be able to take the next step that you want them to do in a way that limits the chance of them being confused or inconvenienced.

Making it easy is one of the most important parts of the process, because each step that you are asking someone to take introduces the possibility that they will abandon the process and move on to something else. By making it easy, you are increasing the chances of them moving from that step to the next, and the more times you can do that, the more people will arrive at the point where they give you money.

To be more specific, it means making it as easy as it possibly can be, not just what *you* would consider easy. Remember, the way you think is different to your prospects. So what you would consider easy isn't going to be what they would consider easy. And you can only begin to start planning to make it easy when you have a good understanding of what they are likely to do.

There is a great story about a water salesman in Mexico who positions himself at the top of a rather steep mountain at a tourist attraction. Every year, countless tourists from around the world underestimate the climb and the heat and are desperate for water.

The story goes that he sells 1L bottles of water for around $20. Supply and demand!

I think about that story when thinking about how the same product can be positioned in different ways and command different fees. The same bottle of water is 50p in a supermarket, £1.50 in a vending machine, £3 in a restaurant, £5 on a plane, £10 at Wembley Stadium, and $20 up that mountain.

But I've always thought this extra point; if that salesperson sold the water in a sealed can, and didn't provide a bottle opener, then it doesn't matter how desperate people are to drink it. He hasn't made it easy.

Every step of your process should be easy to take. That isn't to say you don't want to qualify people, but it should be easy for the people you want to go through the process to do so.

One of the most visual ways in the natural world that this can materialise is *desire paths*. This is the phenomenon whereby a path is created in nature as the unnatural consequence of designers in planning not taking into account what people are likely to do.

As time goes by, the path is eroded by people choosing to walk in the direction they want instead of a potential longer way when architecture is designed without thinking about what is easiest.

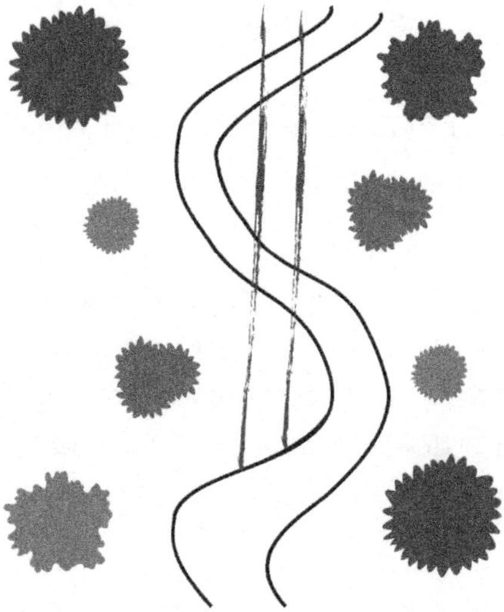

Ohio State University actually designed a large space between buildings as a fully grassed area, and after a year noticed where these desired paths were and paved over them. They allowed the students' behaviours to indicate to them what they were likely to do and made it as easy as possible for them by paving the paths based on their behaviours. Small things like this form a larger picture of what someone's enjoyment is, and their enjoyment is what keeps them coming back again and again.

This often materialises when the cash vs card debate happens amongst business owners.

There is a good amount of businesses that will mandate you use cash only and equally a large amount that mandates card only. These two sides of that coin often have arguments. I generally don't agree with either.

You may side with one argument more than another, whether on a moral stance or a convenience stance. But none of that takes into account what is the easiest thing for your potential customer to do. Much like business owners can fall on either side of that divide, the customers can too.

Take the fantastic example of a takeaway restaurant I encountered. It had far better food than most of the competition around it, with better quality ingredients. But it was cash only and they don't deliver, so people can only order from them by calling up, getting in the car, stopping by a cash point (which isn't close to the restaurant) and getting the right amount of cash out.

Frankly, when someone is in the mood for a takeaway, it is usually because they can't be bothered cooking. And if you can't be bothered doing that, the thought of going out, regardless of weather and those inconveniences versus choosing another takeaway that accepts Apple Pay and can be ordered in two minutes, isn't difficult.

Being fully transparent, the restaurant more than likely wants cash-only purchases because it is easier to account (or indeed incorrectly account) for transactions, but even that doesn't make sense, since they would generate more orders and therefore more profit if they offered other options.

The fact is, your prospects will use any minor excuse to abandon a process. You've already learned that people don't care about the business, and those people naturally won't leap through multiple steps to do the thing you want them to do, unless it is made easy.

You're fighting an uphill battle at every stage; the easier you make that process, the more likely they are to get through and actually do what you want.

So ask yourself this: *How easy is it to give you money?*

People should be able to pay you in almost any way they want. You will make more money if someone BACS transfers; you don't need to worry about processing fees. But if you mandate that, someone has to actively transfer it from their bank, usually manual means. For some that is better, and those should get the details they need either sent to them or have them easily at hand so they can pay. For others, they prefer card, so they should be able to pay by card.

Plenty of clients will want to pay by card because they can get air miles or extra points by doing so, and while that costs you a small fee, it's easier for them. It is a bonus for them to spend money with you; "I can get a free holiday from the air miles in addition to the benefits of your service if I pay in full by card? Where do I sign!" is the kind of reaction you want someone having when paying you money.

Receiving money should be the easiest part of your sales process, and if you are putting barriers up that make it tough for someone to do that, then why?

Whilst the exchange of money should be the easiest part of the process, realistically every step of your process should be easy.

Take referrals. If you regularly get people referring your business because of the amazing experience they had, you want that to be made easy for them. Ideally, you would want them to see a bit of a demo of what you do, for which you should be easily accessible. If someone wants to send a prospect your way to do more business together, excellent. Make it easy for them.

For example, you could have a demo link saved behind a keyboard shortcut so you can type a series of characters on your keyboard that you remember so you can send them that link within seconds of them asking. Most mobile devices have settings whereby you can auto-replace certain things you type with anything, including URLs. You could use the characters "mlnk" as a shortcut for a URL link to book a meeting with you, so whenever someone asks for a call, you have the link ready and easily at hand. The faster you get it to them and the easier it is for them to book, the more likely they will do so.

It is easy for you, and because of that it is easy for the prospect. At the point at which they reach out, they are the most interested they have been, and that interest is only going to decrease over time without the prospect being engaged. If it takes you hours or days to get back to them, the chances of them filling out the form you want them to are naturally lower, so it should be easy for you to deliver what they need as quickly as you can.

This should be in granular detail. Don't think of it from an overview of "I want them to book a meeting," go into more depth and look at the steps. If they are enquiring, how easy is it to get them to engage in the conversation? How easy is it to give them answers to the questions they have? How easy is it for them to know what the next step is? When they are ready to book a meeting, how easy is it for them to do so? How many choices do you give them to make it easy for them to accommodate? When they have booked, how easy is it for them to turn up, get reminders, have expectations set?

That seems like a lot of questions to answer, but you need to make those steps as easy as possible. There will be drop-off at each stage of any process you put in, which is expected. None of that drop-off should be because the next step wasn't easy enough to take.

Almost every technological advancement over the last 20 to 30 years has been driven by increasing consumer convenience. People are naturally looking for an easier way to do the thing they want. Some would call that lazy; I would say it is efficient. Is it lazy to drive somewhere that takes 10 minutes rather than walk there in one hour?

I don't know what year you are reading this book, so the following prediction could be completely off. However, this is being written at the dawn of virtual and augmented reality, and I honestly can't see a world where that isn't commonplace in the future.

I predict that before 2035, you will be able to watch most major sports via virtual reality as if you are in the stadium, with you being able to purchase a package that allows you to access that feed.

Viewing it from the eyes of a football fan who has been around the UK following a usually below-average football team, when I first heard about the ability to view a game in virtual reality, I couldn't see a world where that doesn't happen.

I love seeing a game in person, there is nothing quite like it. But football has a worldwide audience, and allowing them to go through the in-stadium experience in virtual reality (and of course, charging a consumer a nominal fee to access that feed), you'd get people hooked that could never experience it in person.

They will make it easy for football fans to get more out of their experience, and that ease is crucial. Not to mention, if a stadium has 80,000 seats, they can sell 80,000 tickets. But if you can sell an individual stream to one person on virtual reality an unlimited amount of times, that potential for revenue is only capped by the amount of people interested in the sport. And to access it, all they have to do is put on a headset in the comfort of their own home and pay a small fee? That's easy, therefore it's likely.

From a practical perspective, there are a few things you should use to make it easy for potential clients.

Step 1: Collect Data Easily

Make it incredibly easy for a prospect to give you their information. Don't ask a huge amount of questions up front, but put links in every different place they see you. For example, if you are at conferences or exhibitions, have QR codes on your stand, your banners, your brochures, and business cards that you carry round with you. However you communicate with someone, make it easy for you to say "Brilliant, let me get your details, scan here."

If you are sending an email, make sure the call-to-action buttons (the buttons you want them to press) are always in view no matter what they are looking at, so the second they think "This might be something I am interested in," they can press the button immediately.

Step 2: Don't Ask for Too Much

Only ask for the information you actually need at their first point of contact. Rarely would that be more than first name, last name, email, phone number, maybe company name (if you are B2B) and any questions that you definitively need the answer to at an early stage. Anything else you need or want to know, you can ask later; your priority at that stage is to get your information, so make it easy.

You will have seen this yourself, where you have visited a website and are greeted at the start of the process with a form that asks a dozen or more questions, some of which you don't have the information at hand, and you just give up. Most of those questions can be asked later, but at the point where you want them to simply make an enquiry, just ask what you need to.

Also, make that step a bit juicy for them, so your prospect will be giving their information to get something in exchange: either a free download or a demo of something that has piqued their curiosity. We will cover that in more depth in Chapter 12.

Step 3: Make It Engaging

You should make it very easy for your prospect to engage in conversation with you from the first moment they enquire. When someone enquires with you, it would be great for them to get a video sent via WhatsApp within seconds that thanks them for enquiring and states what happens next, while also encouraging them to click on buttons.

These start a conversation with you, even though it is clear everything is automated – and you should make it clear that what they are receiving is automated and designed to improve their experience, while a team member will be in touch soon. The more you get them engaging, the more you have their attention; and the longer you can keep their attention, the more likely they are to get further in your process. So it has to be easy.

To see how easy it can be to get people to engage, send me the word **ENGAGE** on WhatsApp.

Step 4: Make the Next Step Clear

If your next step is a sales call, make it clear the next step is a sales call. This might sound obvious, but remember they don't care about you yet, so they won't make any leaps in their mind to do what might seem logical to you. Make it easy for them to book in, by providing a link or giving them the option to start a live conversation to work out a time that might not be available in the calendar. For that link, you can use your CRM system or calendar management system, and when those calls are booked into the diary, the system should stop following up with the prospects.

Step 5: Meeting Reminder Series

An incredibly important step if you have ever had an issue with people not turning up for meetings that they have committed to. When a prospect has a meeting booked, you should send reminders to them letting them know what the meeting will be at the time they have booked, reminding them why it is happening and offering them the chance to reschedule if plans have changed.

Just before the call is about to start, you should send the location details for the meeting (a video call link, a physical address, etc.) so it is at the top of the prospect's inbox, making it easy to find and removing that as a potential barrier.

Every Step in the Process Should be Easy

Because your prospects don't give a shit about you, anything other than pure ease and simplicity will just discourage them from continuing. They are always looking subconsciously for a reason to give up and look elsewhere, so the slightest bit of effort can point them in another direction.

One positive is that those who aren't as discouraged and are completely enamoured with your product already and are usually ready to buy, will go through the process with the same ease as someone who needs a bit of assistance. So there is no negative for those that are ready, and only positives for those that aren't yet.

Everything comes back to the mentality and perspective of the prospect, and the less they care about what you do the less likely they are to jump through hurdles. They don't know about your business in as much depth as you, so what you think might be an easy step could actually be a massive hurdle in the mind of someone who doesn't care about working with you yet.

It is no coincidence that larger organisations spend millions investing in apps that are easy to use. Amazon introduced a one-click buy button on their site and in their app for the pure purpose of making it easy for you to impulse-buy an item. They are also spending millions year after year to develop Alexa to understand your buying habits and take orders by just saying words out loud in your house. What easier way could there be to order?

Shopify, the large e-commerce website provider, introduced a feature on their sites that allows someone who has checked out one of their sites to create an account and one-click-buy on any other site. That makes it easier for consumers to buy, which means their sites generally have a higher conversion rate – which brings in clients and customers.

If you have ever interacted with a business and thought "Ah, that was easy," rarely has that thought been accompanied by negative emotion. It is almost always positive. You want your prospects to feel positive when dealing with you.

An important part of any business is "social proof", and predominately in the form of reviews. There is a reason Amazon puts the review score and number above the price on their listings; because people would rather spend £15 for an item with 1,000+ positive reviews than £10 on the exact same item with little to no reviews. It's a safe bet. How easy is it for people to review you?

Firstly, are you asking for reviews? Remember, people don't care about you, they generally don't give you positive reviews off their own back without a prompt.

Next, how are you asking for them? Is it a simple message that says, "Can you review me?" because that question not only is a closed question, but you aren't giving context. Have you put a link for them to click once and get to exactly where they need to? Or do they have to search for your company, assume you want the review on Google, find where they need to go and then give you a review?

Businesses assume that sending an email asking for a review is enough to get positive reviews. It might get some, but how easy is it for the client to do so? Even down to what time you are sending the request because if it is within working hours, they are likely to be doing something else that will take priority.

A great way to ask for a review is to do so with a video via WhatsApp that specifically states "I am looking for a favour and hoping you can help. I've set myself targets this year, and to achieve them I need your help to let others know the great service/results they could get.

What do you need from me to steal 30 seconds of your time to click the link below and leave a review for other people?" The link should go straight to your chosen review page, so it is easy for your clients to do it. The video should be sent in the evenings or at a time that you have told them in advance it will be sent. You've asked a personal favour, so ignoring it isn't as easy as it would be ignoring an email.

When looking at what your prospects go through, you need to remember that it should be easy from their perspective. What you find easy isn't necessarily what your prospects find easy.

You are used to your process, you are used to your business. Your prospects aren't.

Take a look at every process you are asking your prospects and customers to go through, and do so in granular detail. What is being sent to them, what steps do you need them to take, and how they take those steps.

Are they doing so on a mobile device? Is it easy to do on a phone?

Are they doing so on a computer? Is it simple to follow on a computer?

Are they doing so in person? Is your signage clear enough?

Spend some valuable time to look at each stage of the process your prospects could drop off, no matter how benign you might think their reason for dropping off, and ask yourself this one crucial question: Is this the easiest thing for them to do? And if the answer is no, change it. Because if it isn't easy, someone who doesn't care about you won't bother.

It borderline needs to be difficult for them to not do the thing you want them to do. Remember, by looking at things from your prospect's perspective, and knowing they don't care about you, that mentality will help work out what needs to be done to make the process as easy as possible.

The biggest bit of advice I can give is that if this is ringing true with you, but looking at those parts of the process is going to be a larger undertaking than you think possible right now, then make it easy for yourself. Look at your diary, and block out some time in a week that you are likely to be quiet on anyway. Don't try and tackle this on a Monday morning if that is often your busiest time. If you're quiet on Wednesday afternoons, then do it there.

If you get distracted easily, then book a space outside of your normal working environment and allocate the time for that. A great tip is to spend money on hiring out a small space - there is nothing quite like the fear of wasting money to kick you up the arse to get you doing the thing you need to.

The easier you make it for you to look at the processes, the easier it will be to tackle. Even if that means spending one day focusing on your sales process, another focusing on your meeting follow-ups, and another focusing on your onboarding.

Once it is easy for you to make those improvements, it will quickly become easy for your prospect journey to improve.

Chapter 5
Occupied Time Is Better Than Dead Time

A widely adopted misconception when it comes to sales processes is that "speed is everything." Sales gurus will tell you this is all that matters.

I disagree.

For clarity, studies have shown that speed is an important part of the process. However there is something more important, and that is what the prospect feels and what their expectations are.

This Chapter will explore why being consistent with experience and setting clear expectations are actually more important, and that, combined with speed, it can be a powerful system that begins the journey of turning your prospects from those that don't give a shit, to those that want to spend money with you.

How Your Prospects Experience Time

By understanding that your prospects' perception of time is significantly more important than the duration of that time, you will be able to cater for the experience you are pushing your prospects through to feel natural and enjoyable.

This is particularly important for those businesses that can't always call their leads within the first few moments of them enquiring, as practical life within the business means that isn't always possible.

There is an amazing example of this that appeared in Houston airport in the early 2010s.

Senior management was concerned about the number of complaints they were receiving as a result of longer waits for baggage to be delivered to the belts following a flight. As there are many different airports people can choose from in Texas, some were opting for other airports further away, because the experience was better. This was costing Houston airport money and reputation. Not to mention, airlines were often getting annoyed passengers were complaining to them instead of the airport itself.

The senior managers looked at the problem the same way most would have and came to the conclusion that they could solve this problem by reducing the wait time. They spent money, investing in new equipment and hiring extra baggage handlers, spent time training them and increasing the team. On paper, it worked; the wait time dropped to eight minutes. Alas, the complaints continued.

They continued because people don't enjoy standing around doing nothing. Think about it: Waiting for bags after you have travelled, sometimes for a long period of time, and often at the end of a holiday, you aren't in the most positive of mindsets. Behaviourally, it is natural that you aren't going to be positive, so being made to stand waiting for a belt to turn on, surrounded by other tired people, and being nearly killed by someone who can't control their baggage trolley, isn't a positive place in the first place.

They thought outside the box and did some research to realise that the gates were one minute from the baggage belts, which meant that people were waiting seven minutes. Seven dead minutes, where they could do nothing other than stand and watch bags from other flights circling belts, almost rubbing it in their faces that their bags were still waiting to arrive.

A consultant came in and suggested one change that solved all the complaints instantly; park the planes further away. That increased the walk to 7+ minutes, and the wait time at the belt was seemingly reduced to hardly any time at all. Instantly, there was no dead time, as it was occupied by the walk.

You see, speed isn't always the answer, but occupying someone's time with clear expectations can nurture them in the interim. I'd argue the same satisfaction would have been achieved if, instead of parking the planes further away, they had a live band playing great music in the baggage hall to entertain people.

Combining the walk with live music and an interesting scenic route would be the best of both worlds. It would also get people actively talking about how great the experience of disembarking a plane is in this airport, thereby not only eliminating complaints but actively turning them into recommendations.

Take the following scenario:

You are waiting at a train station for the next train. In Scenario 1, on the left, you are waiting 5 minutes. However, there is no indication of when the next train will be, no indication on which platform it will be. You don't know the station, there are no staff members or other passengers around you, you don't know if the staff are on strike, and have no signal on your phone to answer any of the questions.

Essentially, 5 mildly anxiety-inducing minutes.

In Scenario 2, on the right, you are waiting 10 minutes. However, you know exactly where you need to be, there is a digital board that tells you when the train is due and counts down, so you are always aware of what is happening. You can easily go to the shops, sit down, relax, and go to the toilet.

Which one are you choosing?

Most people – not everyone – will choose Scenario 2, which is double the time of the first scenario. Of course, there will be exceptions; if someone is late for example, time is the only thing that is important in that moment.

For the most part, the quality of your time is more important than the speed. This applies to almost every business.

If someone puts in an enquiry, getting back to them quickly is important. But what is more important is setting clear expectations and letting them know they are being looked after.

Managing Expectations

Another example of how speed may not be as important as time is when an enquiry comes in between 9pm to 7am.

It would be weird to call them immediately, and would arguably be unprofessional. Therefore someone enquiring at 9:01pm would be waiting at least 10 hours for a response; and that is the best-case scenario, not a realistic normality.

If multiple enquiries come in during that time, unless your team can make calling them their top priority first thing the next working day, your prospects will inevitably be waiting longer. That isn't great.

What is important at that stage is the quality of the expectations being set and how that is delivered. In a later Chapter, we will talk in more depth about expectation setting, but the important point at this stage is that they aren't left thinking, "What happens next?"

To achieve that, here are the three most important things in these scenarios:

1. **Set their expectations**
   This is where you let them know what is going to happen next. If you are always going to get back to them within 24 hours, tell them you will get back to them within 24 hours. Importantly, don't be optimistic, be realistic. So if you usually get back to them within a shorter scale, don't promise that is the norm. As humans, we are great at switching emotions when our expectations have suddenly been unrealised.
2. **Build their trust**
   This is an opportunity to wow them beyond what they were expecting when they first put the enquiry in. If their first enquiry elicits a service-oriented and personal message featuring team members showcasing your professionalism, they

are going to have a much more positive opinion of your business than they would have had before. You are exceeding their expectations, which builds trust. And people buy from people they trust.

3. **Answer their commonly asked questions**
   The biggest detractor of sales failure is when people have unanswered questions and doubts as they progress. This is a chance to address questions you know will commonly come up about your business in a proactive way, and answer them in a way that can progress the sale further along. Remove as much doubt as you can at this stage, and more people will progress to the next step, which you have explained throughout the message.

At the initial contact point from your prospect (form completion, advert response, inbound message, etc.), you have done the hard work of attracting their attention. Marketing is all about getting someone to look at you, and take action in moving towards your business. That form they have completed, that enquiry they've put in, that interest they have shown is the point at which their interest in you is the highest it has ever been. After all, if it had been higher before that point they would have already enquired.

What you really want from that moment is for the prospect to go, "Wow, this is great", and at the very least you don't want their experience to be worsened by anyone thinking negatively. You want them to be impressed since your first impression is everything. Leaving them thinking "What happens next?" isn't an emotion that progresses the conversation.

They don't care about you, so for a split second, you want to give them a little more of a reason to start caring, not less. Blow them away!

You won't achieve that by having a message that says "Thank you for your enquiry, we will be in touch". It needs to be better than that. It needs to occupy their time and set clear expectations.

Occupy Their Time!

Be the walk from the plane to the bags, be the digital board at the train station.

Your job at that first point of contact is to keep them engaged and get them to actively spend more time thinking about you and the business. It would be amazing if that engagement was your team on the phone within seconds, but that isn't practical.

Being told clearly what happens next and then meeting the expectations you set, is the next best thing. For the most part, it's the only practical reality most small businesses have.

Whatever got them to put in that enquiry took a small amount of their time. Those next few moments can be the difference between them taking the next step and them losing interest.

The quality of their occupied time at that stage is vital. It is the first impression that can dictate someone being impressed or someone staying in the mentality that they don't care about your business.

How to occupy their time is going to be down to your business and what you offer, but the best way for you to find out is to ask your clients what they liked and didn't like about your onboarding process, from start to finish. What could you have done better? You can only know that by looking at things from their perspective.

Remember, you won't ever know what sales you are missing because of things that are in your blind spots. Unless every enquiry coming into the business is moving to the next step of your process (which, if we are honest, is unlikely if not impossible), there is something putting them off. The quality of their time right at the start is going to be a big deciding factor in their motivation to get to the next step.

The network of people testing your process will be a great tool to use in making changes to this first point of contact, and telling you what that time should be occupied with.

Your Business...and Dating

It's much like when you go dating: You want to give a great first impression. You likely care about the small things a little more at that stage than two years into the relationship. Turning up to the date on time, listening to the other person, and being polite in general are all things that make more of a difference on the first date, compared to years into your relationship.

If you are in or have been in a committed relationship, remember back to the first time you met. There is always a small thing you remember about that time, compared to further into the relationship where the smaller things aren't as memorable.

If you haven't had that experience, you will remember moments when you first met with friends who told you this is a potential friendship that could evolve.

You are in a long-term relationship with your business, and you need to be treating your prospects as if they are dating it for the first time. What you think is a small thing could be the deciding factor for your business succeeding on that date.

Their experience and quality of time at the start of their interactions with your business should blow them away, and you should communicate effectively with them and let them know what your goals, intentions and expectations are.

If you are saying, "I get back to a lead as soon as possible," you may feel you are doing great. On the surface, that is good service, but in reality that is all focusing on you and not your prospect.

What is fast for you as the business isn't necessarily fast for the potential sale. An enquiry that comes in at 5:05pm on a Friday could have a business going back to them at 9:05am on a Monday. That is 10 minutes in the business world, but it's three days in a prospect's mind. And unless you have the ability to speak with every single lead within minutes, you need something to increase the quality of that time.

This is all important, but it can only do so much. The quality of the build-up to the next step can do a lot of heavy lifting. But if too much time does pass, the prospect will either forget about you, move to your competition, or lose so much trust in your business that they won't want to work with you. And that is starting from a position of them not caring in the first place!

This quality can rarely be done with a manual touch, which is why automation plays a significant part in what your processes should look like. Good thing there is a Chapter on exactly that coming up next.

By occupying your prospect's time with great expectation setting, and doing so immediately at the point of their enquiry – through automation primarily – you can give them the quality of experience that is going to interest and excite even those that don't give a shit about your business!

It is important because once you realise they don't care, that they are a real person, they have natural tendencies to do things in certain ways, and that things need to be made easy for them, you will start to understand how to occupy their time.

Underpromising and overdelivering at every stage is an essential part of keeping someone blown away by what you do. You have competitors, and you need to stand out from them if you want to get the business from your ideal customer. This means more than just setting and meeting expectations, which are the basic experiences your customers go through. It is about nurturing them in a timely manner.

Theme parks have had to learn how to do this over time. One of the biggest detractions people have with going to theme parks is the wait times for the rides. There are benefits to those wait times for the park operators: he longer you are in the park, the more likely you are to spend more money on food and drink, therefore increasing the value of a customer.

But the queues are often the most boring part of the day and therefore the most negative part of people's recommendations.

If all theme parks had queues that were simply lines that doubled back on themselves like airport security, chances are the quality of their experience would lean too much towards the negative to bring someone back.

Since queuing is an inevitable part of the day, they had to improve what would otherwise be seen as a negative experience. Now, most theme parks intertwine the queue with parts of the ride.

They set clear expectations on wait times at the entrance of the queue, which is often overestimating the time (underpromising), and is never less than the time you would have to wait (meeting and exceeding expectations).

When you are in the queue, they generally attempt to make your surroundings an interesting place to be in. Whether that is intertwining it with nature, theming the queue line with the ride itself, having music being played throughout or even actors walking up and down the queue line itself, all of this is designed to occupy your time making your perceived quality of experience higher.

You and your business should adopt a lot of these strategies to impress your prospects. What feels like an inevitable part of the process in waiting for your team to get back to a prospect is the same as the queue in the theme park.

You need their time within that process to be enjoyable. Of course, if you were waiting hours in that queue, it doesn't matter how lovely the experience was. Speed is still a defining factor.

Should their time waiting for your sales team to get back to them be something that overall is positive, they are more likely to be receptive to a call and even book one themselves.

This is critically important because it is one of the areas where small improvements can have a massive impact.

The stage from initial enquiry to speaking to your team for most businesses is the largest drop-off point. Between prospects not answering their phones to not opening emails, not showing up for meetings to ignoring DMs and messages, the improvements at this stage can have such a large impact, that they shouldn't be ignored.

The easiest way to improve the rate at which these prospects drop off in the initial parts is to make their experience a quality one, and occupy their time effectively.

Get this bit right, and you are setting a foundation for your prospects throughout their interactions with your business that is overall positive.

Getting someone who doesn't care about your business to be impressed is the kind of leap in emotions that turns someone from a prospect to a sale.

Chapter 6
Automation Is Not Optional, It's Essential

This Chapter is going to explore why automation is essential to your business. By the end of it, you are going to see that not having it is actually harming how your customers see you, their quality of time and their experience.

Automation allows you to improve the quality of their experience and occupy their time better than any manual process can, which can be one of the biggest improvements you can make.

First, I need to clarify something: *Automation shouldn't replace the human; it should support it.*

A common misconception is that automation lowers the quality of the experience and removes the human-to-human touch, which is overwhelmingly incorrect. Automation done poorly can do that, but when done well it can only be beneficial for everyone; this Chapter will show you how to do it well.

We're specifically focusing on the initial automation that your prospects go through, but the theories we will touch on can cover any element of a prospect's interaction with your business.

By doing this, you can improve their customer experience while saving you time internally to work on the business, rather than in the minutia of repetitive tasks. This is ideal if you are juggling that time and more often than not finding yourself losing the battle between the day-to-day running of the business, and want to spend more time growing the business while also improving customer conversions, retention and referral rates.

You will be able to recall a time in your life when you enquired with a business and were left thinking, "What happens next?" No clarity on the next steps, just a simple message that says, "Thanks, enquiry received" or some other generic message – if you were even lucky enough to be acknowledged.

While remembering that moment, ask yourself this: Did that make you more or less likely to spend money with the business?

Aside from those with a kink around being ignored, chances are you fall into the less likely category.

Imagine doing all the hard work of getting a potential customer to enquire with your business, all that time, money and effort put into marketing. You've done it, they've filled in a form! And their first feeling after that made them less likely to buy from you…

The reality is that most small businesses do this. And those small businesses make up over 99% of all businesses; it's bleak.

Now imagine you enquire with a business and the day after you get sent a box of chocolates and a small gift; you'd be over the moon! This Chapter is about finding the middle ground between what is realistic and what is effective.

The first part of this is what I call "The 0 to 80 Theory."

0-80 is Better Than 0-100

A mistake commonly made in any business implementing big changes and shifts in perspective, is they take on too large of a task at the time. This issue is they try to implement the perfect version of that idea, and as a result, they miss the core of the benefits they could have implemented. I call this the 0-100 problem.

When you are implementing any new changes to the business, you should think of your starting point being the 0 mark, and perfection being 100. It is incredibly important to realise that 100 is impossible, it doesn't exist. Too many business owners get caught up trying to get to perfection before they implement changes. It is one of the primary problems that stifle growth within a business.

That journey from 0 to 100 isn't as simple as it seems. Each step from one number to another isn't the same amount of effort, and it fluctuates.

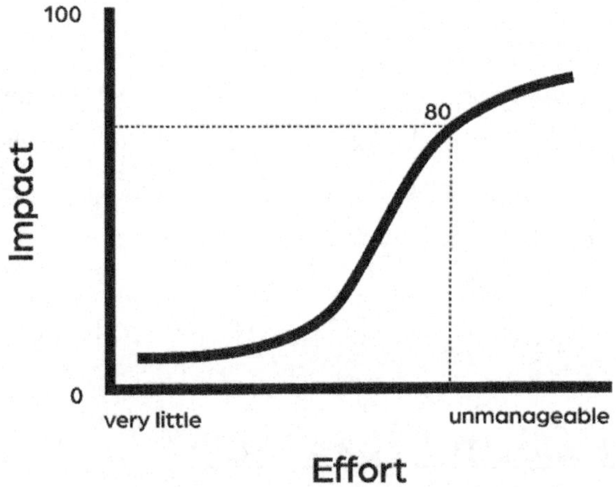

The problem is as follows: If you aim too high, the amount of effort it takes becomes an undertaking that is too large, and eventually you don't even begin. One task becomes five tasks, that becomes 50, that becomes 500 and so on. The thought of doing 500 tasks is more than enough to put you off beginning in the first place, so it just never happens.

You should approach any changes that you put into your business aiming for 80, not 100, so you get the benefit of massively improving the business without being bogged down by the thought of everything becoming overwhelming.

The best way to visualise exactly what this can look like is to think of launching a restaurant. The 0 point is where the building is just a shell of what it can look like. 99 is a Michelin-star restaurant that is booked out for months ahead of time.

Everyone wants to get to 99, but doing that is a mammoth task, and trying to do it all at once is incredibly rare. But you could have a very successful thriving restaurant that doesn't have a Michelin star, and that should be the aim. That is the 80.

In reality, each step along the journey to 100 takes a different amount of effort and has a different level of impact on your business. There comes a point where extra effort doesn't actually mean a noticeable impact on the business.

Your first step is fitting out the kitchen, with the equipment that makes the lives of the chefs easy or difficult. The effort to pack that out and the financial investment can range wildly, but most guests won't notice a huge difference. Lots of effort, not much impact, and that is the 0-30 range.

One difficulty is that when a business starts a project, the effort they put into going from 0-30 not having the large impact they want can sometimes lead to them getting discouraged before they even see the impact of the work they do. Never underestimate the impact of a poor mindset from a business owner on the success of their endeavours.

Truth is, 30-80 is where the real impact comes. In this example, this is where you choose the menu, source your ingredients, decorate the restaurant with a standard collection of colours, hire good staff, and advertise out to the local area in your standard ways. This leap, done well, can make or break the business.

Your 80-85 step is refining that menu, sourcing better ingredients, and spending extra time deciding what colour the walls should be instead of going for basic white. It could also include adding extra menus for different days and specialty dining, upgrading the staff uniforms, and adding a little gift at the end of the meal for guests to take home. These are all things that will make a difference, but the effort/investment is large in comparison to the improvement. It is an improvement, so there is an incentive to make the steps from 80-85. There comes a point where any extra effort will have a minimal impact on the prospect and the chances of them buying.

85-90 is investing in dedicated staff training programs, expanding your marketing beyond the standard strategies and thinking a little outside the box, investing in loyalty schemes to bring people back, hiring staff in admin roles and marketing positions instead of diluting those responsibilities to existing members of staff. Again, a lot more effort and there is a noticeable benefit, but it is a big leap in effort and something that takes a lot more consideration. For that business, does their idea of a successful restaurant necessitate the extra effort to get to that increased impact? That is for them to decide.

From 90 to 99, each incremental step is a large leap in effort, and those individual steps can have an impact but sometimes those bits are nuanced and lost on some customers. This is how you go from a successful restaurant to one that people will actively travel hours on end to experience.

The simple fact is the effort it often takes to go from 80 to 100 is much more than the effort required to go from 0 to 80. The problem is most businesses are so transfixed on getting as close to 100 initially that the level of effort they have to put in is daunting. Generally, that is what holds people back from making the changes needed to improve. But the biggest impact you can have is the jump from 0 to 80, and if you focus on that, you can grow the business massively in a small space of time.

Websites are a great example of this, and an example of where your time should be allocated. A website should be functional, easy to use, fast and a great representation of your business. Design is important, although often functionality is the more important element. One big part of the effectiveness of a website is how fast it is; the slower a website loads the faster people will abandon the process.

If a website takes 15 seconds to load, getting that down to three seconds usually isn't a massive task, it is just small changes. Getting it to go from one second to 0.8 seconds is often a lot more complicated, so the effort is much higher. The impact for most people will be a lot more obvious when they see a website go from 15 seconds to three, rather than seeing it speed up from one second to 0.8 seconds. Major companies like Amazon will see a difference in the latter improvement, so the added effort and expense make sense to them. But for most people reading this book, it is not worth the extra effort. Unless you are reading this Mr. Bezos, in which case we should have a call!

If a business started at the 15-second mark and wanted to get to 0.8 seconds, the size of that task would be put off over and over. But in delaying it, you are missing out on the benefit of getting to three seconds.

By planning out your changes to take you from 0 to 80, you are making the task a lot less daunting and more feasible to enact, and in doing so you are getting the core of the improvements in place. You are making it easy for yourself to implement the changes, and making it easy is important. Then once you are at 80, you can look at getting closer to 85, 90 and beyond. But without doing the hard work of getting to 80, you'd never get there in the first place, because 80 gives you a solid foundation for success.

A great example of this is sending gifts to clients when they sign up with you for your services. While writing this book, one of the tasks I have set myself is to create a gift that I will send to new clients when they come on board for my 1-to-1 packages.

I have found a local business that is part of the community that creates stunning homemade chocolates and have created a variety box specifically for this offering. I told them a budget, they put together a box and printed a small sticker on the front to brand the box as mine, and included the option for a handwritten letter. That entire offering is going from 0 (where nothing was being sent) to 80, which will impress my clients. If I left it like that, it would be amazing and have a great impact.

The company even took my branding colours and chose packing paper that matched the brand as closely as possible. That was the 80 to 85 jump.

I then tasked my graphic designer with creating a box-sized sticker that could go on the front, with my logo and a little note about it being a surprise. On the inside of the box cover is a similar-sized sticker with a message from me, thanking them for becoming clients and what their signing up means to me. That is me taking it from 85 to 90.

Because that work has been done, all I need to do now when a new client comes on board is to message the business with the address it needs to be delivered, which minimises the effort but maximises the effect.

Our designer for The Marketing Autopilots is amazing because she can also point out things that most people won't notice. The colour of the box is slightly different to the colour of the business' core branding, and the sticker on the box will show a slight difference. She suggested instead of getting the company to print the stickers, they would look better as custom-coloured vinyl that we could print in bulk ourselves, and send them to the company. She is correct, in that it would be better, but the extra effort isn't going to have a big enough impact on the effect it creates and the purpose of the box in the first place.

No one is going to receive that box with the message and say, "It was an amazing touch, but I wish the colours were the same." That jump could be the 90-91 leap, and the business decided that it isn't the right thing to do to add the effort at each stage, for a benefit hardly anyone will notice.

That attention to detail is great for a designer, and it is why all of our company branding, printing and physical marketing is on point – from my stands, brochures and tablecloths. Overall, there will be areas where it makes a difference, but there is a time and place to pick the battles that take you to 90+ since the biggest impact is found going from 0 to 80.

I implore you to think about what that process looks like for you, and what you should be doing to get to 80, without getting distracted by going beyond before you are there.

If you are planning out your customer journey, having a set generalised structure for all inbound enquiries will take you from 0 to 80. Duplicating that structure and tailoring the initial message in the series for each individual vertical (such as social ads, Google, organic searches, referrals, etc.) ensures that the prospect's first impression is specific to the campaign they came from. This refinement can take you from 80 to 90.

Having each message in the series be unique for the specific ad, campaign and general source might get you from 90 to 99, but will that have a great impact on the success of the campaign? Probably not. Therefore you need to decide as to whether it is worth the very large effort to get there.

When it comes to automation, it will never be as good as a human being there live, speaking to a prospect directly. However, having someone employed 24 hours a day, 7 days a week to call a lead within 60 seconds of them coming in, day and night, might sound like perfection on paper. But in reality, it wouldn't work for a variety of reasons, even after you get past the inevitable labour regulatory issues!

Some businesses get carried away with automations, where they fall down a rabbit hole of possibilities on what can be automated, and layout a task that would take their automation to the 99 mark. The problem is that they never start that task, because the size of the undertaking is often too daunting.

What people can do manually at that initial point of enquiry can very often be unreliable and inconsistent, whereas automating it can be a much more effective process, and often a better one for your prospect.

How Can Automation Truly Benefit Your Business?

Automation is anything that can be triggered to happen as a result of something else happening, without manual intervention from a human being.

This could be as simple as someone filling out a form and a notification being sent to the team, to a highly detailed series of communication channels and chatbots through WhatsApp that get your client engaging.

For the purposes of this book, we want to use the elements of automation to get your customers from a perspective of not giving a shit, to being impressed, feeling looked after and open to doing some business together.

For most businesses, automation can't replace a good salesperson, and nor should it. However, with automation, that salesperson will convert more and have a much easier time of things, as well as your long-term client relationship being a much nicer environment to be in.

Another thing that may be blindingly obvious, is that automation is only a part of the equation, as it needs to have the right feel, messaging, placement, timing, platform and a whole host of other variables to work effectively. I lean quite heavily into WhatsApp and email automation, as it is typically the best received and most effective for me and my clients, while the theories discussed will cover anything that can be automated.

Finally, there are some things that shouldn't be automated. As I write this book, the evolution of AI is growing at an exponential rate, and I currently believe whilst there would be a way to program an AI video call to handle objections in a sales process, you still need that human-to-human connection for sales. People buy from people, and that trust is something much easier garnered by a good connection between prospect and business.

The Automation Workflow

The basic premise of automation is triggers, actions, time delays and filters. They are generally presented as a chronological "flow" that spreads over a period of time.

Triggers

Triggers are something that happens at a moment in time. This could be a prospect filling out a form, responding to an ad, sending you a message, opening an email from you, booking a discovery call, downloading something, watching a video, etc. Anything they are doing to show an interest in what you do, or indeed show disinterest. For some of those actions you will need to have collected their data at some point in the past, and some of those triggers would be the point at which a prospect gives you that data, but all of them can be effective initial triggers.

These triggers can also be internal, from noting in a client file that they have moved from one stage of your sales process to another, uploading documents to that file, ticking boxes internally to send information that has been requested, filling out your own forms etc. These triggers require a manual step for you internally, but can often be a lot more tailored to the prospect based on information you have gathered.

Actions

Actions are simply what happens after something has been triggered, and whilst many systems have a variety of different actions, the most popular ones used are sending communications (WhatsApp, email, SMS, etc), updating files, creating opportunities in a sales pipeline, updating a client, triggering notifications, communication between systems, updating reporting systems, adding specific tags, as well as many others.

Whilst you can have triggers that only trigger one action, they are most effective when multiple actions happen as a result of one trigger

Time Delays

Time delays are fairly self-explanatory, but they generally fall into one of two categories: simple time delays and event-based time delays.

Simple delays are putting a step in that delays the next action for a certain amount of set time: 10 minutes, one day, two months, for example.

These can also be set to only run within certain hours, so you could have a time delay of 24 hours that only actions the next step of the automation within working hours. This is great for communication steps when someone has enquired outside of normal hours and you want to respond only within normal hours.

Importantly, these delays are based on when the trigger occurs.

Event-based time delays are based around a different time, which can either be a universal time specific to that automation. For example, if you are running an offer that expires on a specific date, you might want messages going out to anyone who signed up for that offer in the build-up to the end of the offer, regardless of when they actually signed up.

These can also be based around a time specific to the user, and the easiest analogy is when a prospect books a meeting, that time and date is the event the time delays are based on. And you can build a reminder series around that time specific for that one person.

Filters

Filters are incredibly useful and add a layer of personalisation (as well as complexity) to your automations. With most systems, we can use filters to segment audiences that may well be actioning things based on what information we have on them.

For example, the follow up automation will be different for someone who has enquired about a product and has stated they are ready to buy now, compared to someone who has stated they are thinking about buying in the next six months.

This is often where we take the 0-80 improvement above the 80 mark.

Flows

Flows are the sequence of these events that happen, usually in chronological order, that allow you to lay out all of the elements above. They are occasionally called workflows, journeys, sequences and other variants, depending on the system you use.

Pulling all of this together, you can build a simple example like the following:

> Prospect 1 fills out an enquiry form on a website/landing page **(trigger)**, which in turn alerts the team, and sends the prospect a WhatsApp video thanking them immediately, and an email with all the information **(actions)**. It also updates the system to create a file, adds their information, creates an opportunity in the sales pipeline if they haven't already got one in the system **(filter)**, raises a task for the team to call, adds the tags "website enquiry", "campaign XX" & "new lead", and removes them from the cold advertising audience that sent them to the website in the first place **(more actions)**.

This process aims to get them to book a discovery call with the sales team, and if that was to happen they would be removed from this specific automation flow. For this example, we are mapping out what happens if they fail to book that call.

> After sending the first messages instantly, 24 hours pass **(simple time delay)** and a follow-up message is sent as more of a personal introduction to the team. Should a call not be booked, a further message is sent

72 hours later **(time delay)** which is different whether they have opened the previous messages **(filter)** that asks what questions they have.

This flow is very simple and will be drastically different from business to business, but is a bare minimum for an initial enquiry. It is also a frighteningly overlooked part of the customer experience for most businesses that makes a huge difference in whether they turn up, and what their expectations are.

Why is Automation Essential?

Simply put, this flow can do a lot of the work in answering questions your prospect may have, but the biggest impact is setting expectations.

In the last Chapter, you learned about how people are less worried about the time something takes and more concerned about being informed and having expectations set. The quality of how their time is occupied is essential, and automation can make them consistent and as high-quality as possible.

The point at which a new enquiry comes in is the point where that lead is the most engaged and interested in you. After all, if they were more interested in the past, they would have already enquired. Whilst they still don't care about you and the business, something has caused them to have their interest piqued, and they have taken an action – well done!

This is our chance to WOW them, blow them away and show how impressive your product or solution can be. Your first contact point should do three things:

1. Set clear expectations on what happens next
2. Build trust in the business, and
3. Answer questions they will almost always have.

Setting expectations almost eliminates the question, "What happens next?" which we already know has only negative connotations.

Building trust with your business is essential. When was the last time you gave money willingly and happily to someone you didn't trust?

Answering questions is the toughest part, because there will be unique questions, but every business I have ever interacted with will have some questions everyone asks. And whilst some prospects will ask those questions, a good portion of them won't go out of their way to ask.

For those kinds of prospects, we want to either answer those questions, for which I use an automated instant WhatsApp video, or make it incredibly easy for them to click on buttons to get instant access to those answers.

If you have a prospect that is impressed with the service and the messages coming through, clearly knows what happens next, has an increased level of trust in your business, has little to no unanswered questions at that point, and can see clearly what they have to do next, you are in a much better place than if they simply filled out a form and saw the message, "Thanks, we'll be in touch."

"But Chris, a human can do all of that better than automation can!"

This is a great point. And whilst technically correct, it is rarely as simple as that.

This is where the previous annoying sentence "I get back to leads as soon as I can" comes back. Part of the reason I don't like it is because it is very one-sided, but the main part is that it is so rarely immediate.

If you are a solo entrepreneur, or in a sales team with a small number of salespeople, the practicality of getting back to a lead manually within moments of them enquiring is tiny. Pretending that that is the standard is unrealistic and poor service for the prospect.

The amazing part about putting automation into the process is that you can still have the quality that automation can bring, whilst also getting in touch with those prospects you can call quickly. You aren't doing this in place of what would be great manually, you are doing it in addition.

The Business Resource We All Need

Time is the only resource no business can have any more of.

We'd love to have more time. Businesses can hire more people and have more workable hours, but that doesn't mean they get more time.

Putting that aside for a second, even if we had someone on hand to get in touch as soon as a lead came in, they still can't respond as quickly as automation can!

Take this example:

A 2 minute WhatsApp video is delivered to enquiries within 10 seconds of them clicking "submit" on a form. If that was being done manually, and the person in the video could start recording the video within 5 seconds of the lead coming in (practically impossible), it would still take 2 minutes more to get sent than if it was automated!

All of this does not take into account any leads that come in outside of normal communication hours. This may be 9am to 5pm for your business, it often is slightly earlier and a lot later for most solo entrepreneurs.

However if a lead comes in at 1am, it would be odd if you sent them a personalised video in the dark at home lying in bed. Not to mention, it would definitely irritate any partner you had. That previous sentence is proudly sponsored by Lived Experience!

An automated video allows you to start with "Hi, this is an automated video just to say thanks for…", and you immediately resonate with the prospect regardless of the time they may have enquired. The prospect will instantly have an understanding that you are sending the video as part of customer service and that you are here to help, which builds trust, sets expectations and answers a lot of questions – covering all the parts of the automation we want covered.

Another common misconception that automation can help with is what I like to call the "Why are they always free?" problem. This is the problem whereby if you are automating and pretending to be a human, the prospect may ask the question "If they are successful, how do they have the time to message me instantly?"

The best example of this is a gardener who thinks they are offering a great service by being available on hand all the time.

The gardener offered to come round the day of the enquiry as he was in the area, which isn't an immediate red flag, so generally not a negative! So far, so good. Now, imagine the job they did wasn't amazing but wasn't poor enough for you to not be interested in keeping them on.

Now imagine you ask them about booking in for every month.

The response they give is: "Just give me a ring when you want it done and I'll either be round that day or the following day." To them, they were offering great service. To you and your house, you have to ask, "Why are they always free?" In theory, you want to use a company or individual that is in demand, because if they are good they will likely be in demand. Money isn't always the issue, you just want the garden to be sorted and look great. It begs the question:

How can you be successful and good at what you do, while also *always* having the following day free? That doesn't make sense, and brings in the biggest of killers to a sales process: doubt.

You may have seen this with restaurants. If you are booking a table for a Friday or Saturday night for a restaurant that is new to you, and you call through the day before and the server says, "You can pick any time you want, we have all times available," that says less about it being great service and more about the lack of people booking the restaurant on a weekend.

Remember previously when I said that people do one of three things, one of which is they do what they think everyone else is doing? This has a positive side of course, but also a negative: They won't do what they think no one else is doing.

We generally have a herd mentality; people tend to follow others, but they are also generally hesitant to be the only person going against the grain. Why has no one else booked a table? What is causing people to stay away? Why has the gardener not gotten regular bookings? None of these questions make a prospect more likely to spend money.

Automation can help with this by nurturing a prospect without them having those questions. If the first point of contact is automated and states, "This is automated," while also bringing a prospect further along that sales journey, they never have the question, "Why are they always free and able to call me within seconds of me enquiring?"

You can also help engineer this problem with automation in other ways and create an almost artificial lack of availability. You can do this by having specific days for specific tasks and meetings.

Specific days for different types of tasks can be a game changer in your business. Take sales, for example. As a solo entrepreneur you have to balance your time between tasks that grow the business and tasks that run the business. This is a difficult balance at the best of times. By allocating certain days for sales calls, you can stack back-to-back sales calls in your diary.

This has the incredible effect of putting you in the right mindset at the start of that day, so all you are focusing on is bringing in sales. You are in the best place for your prospects as you aren't distracted by any other meetings that have happened on the day. And just like London buses, when you get one sale coming in, more follow. This isn't a coincidence, this is because you are approaching the day from a place of abundance.

What it also allows you to do is not look like you are always available for calls, and being that free for meetings is often a negative.

This isn't about using the automation dishonestly, and you will hear me saying, "Do not lie to your prospects" at every opportunity I can. This structure simply allows you to do a better job. For me, the automation side allows me to remove a lot of those doubts before I ever actually do something.

Automation is an essential part of the process, but you should still be doing some of the leg work when it comes to your prospects. If you are currently calling them within 48 hours of the lead coming in, you should still do that. The automation can simply allow them to book a time that suits them and set the expectation that if they don't book that time, you will be getting in touch within 48 hours.

The automation supports you in the process and doesn't replace you.

It can cause them to book a call, skipping that step for you and replacing that element of the process. It can also set the expectation of a call making it more likely that they pick up. However, it simply progresses to the next step where human involvement remains essential.

Automate where possible, but delegate or handle tasks yourself where necessary.

Chapter 7
Be Persistent, Not A Pest!

This may be a frustrating Chapter for many, as it focuses around actually showing up and being persistent. However, I want to make it clear that there is a difference between being persistent and being a pest. For some, this can be a fine line.

By the end of the Chapter you will have an appreciation that your business is a constant work in progress, and covering all the bases by being persistent is the only real guaranteed way to be successful. This will be a poignant Chapter for those who are holding back deliberately and are scared of bugging their leads because the shift in mindset will show you that if you aren't being persistent, you are actually offering them poor service.

Ultimately, too many businesses give up on their prospects for a variety of reasons, and very often down to incorrect and misplaced assumptions.

As you've learned already in great depth, your prospects don't care about you. This means that you need to work harder and have a more persistent follow-up process to get them to turn into a sale. Clearly, there will be some exceptions, some people who are ready to go and buy who are often more dominant in personality profile, and we should be ready for that. But generally, they just don't care.

While understanding this assumption is a frustrating realisation, once you do accept it, you realise that the reason people aren't getting back to you is often not the assumption we typically go to, which is, "They just aren't interested."

Ask yourself this: How many times in the past have you wanted to engage with a business, but because it wasn't a priority you gave up initially? And because they never reached back out again, you didn't bother contacting them again?

The reality is, very often we just need a push in the right direction, and that will be down to being persistent.

A study on salespeople and their closing statistics found that 92% give up after facing four or fewer negative responses. In fact, 44% give up after just one negative response.[5]

Frankly, this statistic should blow your mind. It means that only 8% of salespeople are persistent enough to try more than four times to generate a sale from the sales prospect. However, that statistic alone shouldn't completely alter your perception.

The same study found that 80% of consumers are likely to give a seemingly negative response four times before they buy. This means 80% of sales are usually closed by just 8% of salespeople. That is an *enormous* gap.

The most talented and successful salespeople will tell you that a big part of what they do is they are persistent. Yes, they can have skills in sales and know the right things to say, but often the real difference between them and the next salesperson is persistence.

When you remember that no one cares about you, and your leads are human beings as we learned from the early Chapters, you start to realise there are plenty of reasons someone has dismissed your call or pushed a meeting. In fact, there are more reasons that have nothing to do with them not being interested that are often the reasons for not buying at that particular time.

You could call a prospect who has already made their mind up to buy from you and someone who needs what you offer. But if you call them in the middle of something more important, they either don't answer or their response will likely come across as less than positive.

When you realise that people have lives outside of their relationship with you, you understand that their seemingly cold response is likely for another reason entirely. And at this stage, their relationship with you isn't important at all

Now, it is important to clarify that I don't mean calling someone every couple of hours. I also don't mean ignoring if they do tell you they flat-out aren't interested. Being persistent still needs to be done well, and shouldn't waste your time.

Giving Someone An Out

You need to make it hyper-easy for someone who genuinely isn't interested in you to let you know. Some think about this from a reverse psychology perspective, and whilst there is some truth to that, the focus of this is less nuanced than that.

When you reach out to someone whom you have been persistently talking to for a while, and you need clarity on whether they are interested, you should give them an out, that should often sound like the following:

"As I haven't heard from you, I need to make sure I am not being a pest, so if you aren't interested in any way then now is your chance to tell me, I won't take it personally. If however, it is something you feel you would benefit from, let's get some time booked in for our next step. Which would you prefer?"

Or you can try something like this, which stands out a little by being funny:

"I am sending you a message simply to see if you are still interested in doing some business together, or not. If not, send me a picture of a pineapple, and if there is an opportunity to work together, give me a thumbs-up emoji."

A lot of business owners say, "They haven't got back to me, of course, they aren't interested." However, if it is framed like above, the default position is they must still be interested in some way. As I've detailed previously, you've made it incredibly easy for someone to tell you they aren't interested and it isn't right for them. Why would they not tell you at that stage? Chances are, they are interested, and you simply need to get them at the right time.

Being persistent while giving someone the chance to tell you they aren't interested is purely your being in service of the people that you are speaking to. And you will be surprised at how many people come back to you and say,

"Oh we are interested, sorry for not responding, you're right let's book some time in."

This is where the reverse psychology point comes in. People love to feel that they are in control. As you are potentially removing the benefit of your product/service from them, that is often enough to prompt a response.

How do you avoid being a pest? It's a good question. The short answer is simple: Don't act like one.

The longer answer is that if you are approaching your follow-up from a perspective of desperation and just a money-lust position, then you *will* come across as a pest. Desperation doesn't give someone the opportunity to tell you they are not interested. It is a position that is fearful of the answer if they say no. Being in a position of abundance means whether they say yes or no won't make a difference, you just need to know the answer. People sense that.

The great Matt Elwell from the Elite Closing Academy teaches this incredibly well, and one thing that flipped in my mind when educating myself with his teachings was the following:

If your product or service genuinely helps your prospect, by either solving a problem or bringing them joy, you are doing them a disservice by not following up in a persistent way.

It was a moment when I realised I was scared of being rejected by not being persistent in my follow-up because I was worried about them saying no. But actually, they are just humans who have their own lives. And as long as I can genuinely help them, and I am giving them the opportunity to professionally tell me to bugger off if they don't feel I can help. So my not reaching out to them persistently is poor customer service.

If you are ever scared of calling someone again or adding a pitch to your presentation, and you feel a little wrong doing so, ask yourself the following questions:

1. Does your product/service genuinely help people? If yes, ask:
2. Would your prospect benefit from working together? If yes, ask:
3. By holding back the information and opportunity to work together because of your own hesitations or insecurities, are you helping your prospect or hindering their chance of getting that benefit?

Once you ask these three questions, you realise that by not following up and not being persistent, you are preventing them from benefiting from you. That isn't good service; that isn't how to help your prospects.

Remember the question you were asked at the start of this Chapter around an experience you have had with a business where you wanted what they offered, and you simply gave up because of the lack of follow-up? The majority of the time, you would have wanted to buy from them to benefit you in some way.

Maybe they solved a problem you have, maybe they made things easier for you, or perhaps it got you further along in your business. Whatever the reason, them not following you up has led to a delay in the benefit you would have had. Their lack of follow-up has cost you that solved problem, made things harder for longer or held you back in your business.

Good salespeople follow up more than others. Simple as that.

Once you've overcome that mindset, the practically difficult part comes in.

Following Up Persistently

Time is the one resource we can't have more of. It is the most valuable thing we have as human beings.

If you were offered £10 million tomorrow, you would probably take it. If you were offered £10 million tomorrow but you won't wake up next week, you'd say no, because your time is more valuable than money.

Being more persistent with your prospects often means more time being allocated to them and that follow-up.

This can either seem daunting or borderline impossible, and the rest of this Chapter can help.

A lot of your follow-up process can be automated, in a way that mimics what is a behaviourally natural reaction your prospects will have.

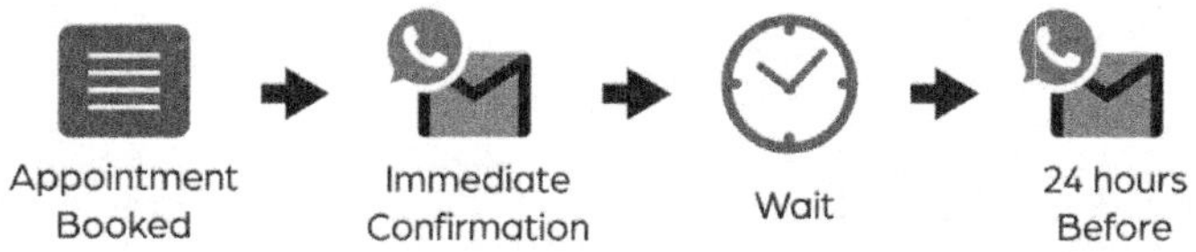

An incredibly effective automation I would recommend you implement is a video that is sent 24 hours before a sales call, that details what will happen on the call, encourages them to let you know if they can't make the call, lets them know what the next steps would be if they were to decide to work together, and asks them questions about the business that they can answer in advance.

That automation for me personally has meant I have a less than 2% no-show rate on sales calls, with a 50% high-ticket conversion rate on all viable leads.

People only don't show up for meetings they have booked because they either have doubts, feel you aren't going to provide them the value they expected when they first booked, or in rarer cases a genuine reason they couldn't avoid. Bar the latter, you can mitigate the other reasons with automation.

That 2% figure makes some business owners gasp, but it is so low because the persistent follow-up message series in the build-up to the meeting makes sure the prospect knows exactly what happens, what value they will gain from attending the meeting and framing how they can proceed to work with people.

If I wasn't persistent, I'd have fewer people turning up to meetings, and therefore less sales.

To see an example of my messages that are persistent but not necessarily a pest, send me the word **PERSISTENT** on WhatsApp.

Another effective automation I would recommend is a WhatsApp message that is sent to a prospect 10 minutes after they open a proposal if more than seven days has passed since you last spoke. That way when a prospect is looking at your proposal in their own time, you can automatically send a message simply saying, "I see you looking! Only joking, but I did just get notified you have opened the proposal I sent over. Generally, this means you are at one of three points: Either you love it and are ready to sign and work together, you have questions, or you have decided you aren't interested. The last option wouldn't usually lead you to open the proposal (I say hopefully), so which describes you best right now?"

It seems a little cheeky of course, but you would be surprised by the lack of negative responses from that message. More often than not, you get a laugh, which is something that, in a sales process, goes down very well.

You can do this by using software that creates a proposal and hosts it online, giving you data and analytics on when it has been opened, and connecting that with CRM systems that can trigger messages based on the automation trigger point (when the proposal is opened), and a time delay of 10 minutes.

It takes time to build trust with people, especially if what they are investing in with you is more of a considered purchase. That time is behaviourally natural, it is what a human does. Trying to force or persuade them to go against what is natural isn't going to be the most effective use of your time.

Being persistent for the right reasons, in the right manner, at the right times is only ever going to be in service of your prospects, which naturally leads to more sales.

Some people will think that any follow-up is going too far, and generally, that is because they have had negative experiences with poor follow-up processes. That, or they are such a dominant personality that they only ever make decisions quickly so the notion of people taking their time is completely alien to them.

Take the example of a DJ arguing about his follow-up. It was with a mobile DJ who specialised in weddings, and he was talking about following up on quotes. He said plainly that once he sends a quote, he never follows it up. This is because, "If they were interested they would buy from the quote, there is no point following up."

A wedding DJ is hired by a couple getting married 99% of the time. That couple is looking at dozens of suppliers they have to get organised for a wedding, from venues, cakes, dresses, and suits, to photographers, videographers and table planners.

When it comes to wedding suppliers, they will rarely just enquire with one. So in this scenario, most people he will be quoting will be speaking to other DJs and/or bands. His presumption was either that they were just going to pick the DJ based on the price and he couldn't impact another supplier's price, or that if they liked and preferred him, then they would just book.

He incorrectly assumed that they cared about him and couldn't fathom that they don't give a shit. In reality, they cared about the wedding night, the entertainment, and the enjoyment of their guests. And the reason people spend extortionate amounts on weddings is because that day is often the most special and intricately planned night of their lives. So going for the cheapest option on those days is rarely the go-to. For some it might be, but do you really want to go for the client that wants the cheapest option?

Someone then suggested to this DJ, "What if there were four other suppliers speaking to your prospects, and one supplier was following up, checking in with them to make sure they had things planned, helping them with any extra information they need to make a decision, offering them conversations on the quote if they had any questions?" Not only were they more likely to win the business, but they are also offering much better service. And do people generally pay more or less for better service? Exactly.

As this book continues, you will see that once you apply the logic that your prospects don't care about what you are doing yet, are real people who act in certain ways, need things made easy for them, appreciate the quality of their time, and don't mind things being automated as long as they are in service of what they are looking to achieve, you'll start to see better results.

By being persistent where it makes sense, you'll turn those leads into sales and happier clients.

With that point being made, you might want to note down my guide below for better sales.

My 5-Point Guide on How To be Persistent Without Being a Pest

1. Ensure you can actually help them.
If you are just following up with someone again and again to try and get their money without a clear understanding that you can benefit them, then you very quickly start falling into unethical selling. You need to offer them something they need and would benefit from, and make sure they have recognised that fact and have indicated it to you before you move forward.

2. Spread it out.
Every business is different, and their consideration towards what you do may take longer or shorter than others. If you have an event you are selling tickets for, and the event is in two weeks, your follow-up is likely going to be more condensed than someone who is selling a house, which typically takes months if not longer. Work out what time periods are natural in your industry and lean into them.

3. Give them an out.
For your own sanity more than anything else, you want to only be talking to prospects who are actually interested and have demonstrated so. If you have given someone the option to tell you they aren't interested again and again, and they still continue to refuse to tell you, there is a good chance they will work with you in the future. If you don't

give them that out, they will lie to you to get out of the awkward conversation of saying no.

4. Be unique and varied.

If you've read this Chapter and your idea of a follow-up is an email that says, "Hi, just checking in, do you want to buy my stuff yet?" then you aren't on the right track. Send a voice note or a personalised video, call them, DM them on socials, comment on their social media posts, support them, and interact with them. Do something to stand out in their mind outside of being between 15,000 other emails all trying to do the same thing. A lot of this can be automated too, as long as it is done well, which we will cover in the next Chapter.

5. Tell them you will be persistent.

In a later Chapter, I will cover the next step's principle in more depth. Needless to say it is a lot more effective when following up with someone when they know it is coming. When you see me at conferences and scan anything I have, there is a follow-up series you enter. That series I let you know about well in advance, so when you receive my persistent follow-up the emotion is, "That is what Chris said would happen" instead of "What does he want now?" This puts me in a much healthier position.

The main takeaway from this Chapter should be that you currently aren't anywhere near as persistent as you should be.

And by not being persistent, you are actually doing your prospects a disservice.

How to automate that is where you can take your follow-up game to the next level without overwhelming your entire business: by adding hours of extra sales tasks.

Chapter 8
The 3 Ps Of Automation

Previous Chapters have covered how automation is an essential part of the process when nurturing your leads. We also discussed how important it is to not replace the human in the process but rather use automation to support that. This Chapter will begin to cover the mechanics of how to do this properly.

This is particularly important when avoiding the perception that something automated is impersonal and frustrating for your prospects to interact with. You as a business want to maintain professionalism throughout, and doing it correctly using what you have learned in the Chapter will be the difference between your customer's experience being fluid and enjoyable vs. being frustrating and unnatural.

One of the main points of reluctance business owners say when it comes to automation is, "My clients don't want automation; they want a real person."

This isn't incorrect, but equally, it isn't the whole picture. People don't want to receive something automated when it is in place of a human or it is trying to pretend to be one.

It is why framing automation is incredibly important, and when framed correctly, automation is both very effective and a better service to your prospects.

Framing is simply where we set expectations with the prospect that this automation is for a specific purpose, and it is there to benefit them. They will have the opportunity to speak to a human, to get there faster and be respectful of their time. This step of automation will help everyone.

Take automation in the context of deliveries to your home.

No one complains about the automated messages they receive to tell them when a package is being delivered. They see these as a great reminder and part of an effective service. In fact, they would often complain if they didn't have the information at hand because uncertainty in any process isn't something we as humans enjoy. But they will dislike it when those automations are erroneous or have information that isn't clear. As a result, this causes them to stay at home waiting for a package for longer than needed or expecting a package that doesn't arrive.

Another example is when you order from a restaurant. A customer won't complain about a restaurant asking for a review after a takeaway has been delivered, and will often take an extra step to leave a review. They will however be incredibly annoyed if the automation still sent a message if the food either didn't arrive or the restaurant cancelled the order.

Automations done well, and in the right manner, will be received well. This is where the Three Ps come in.

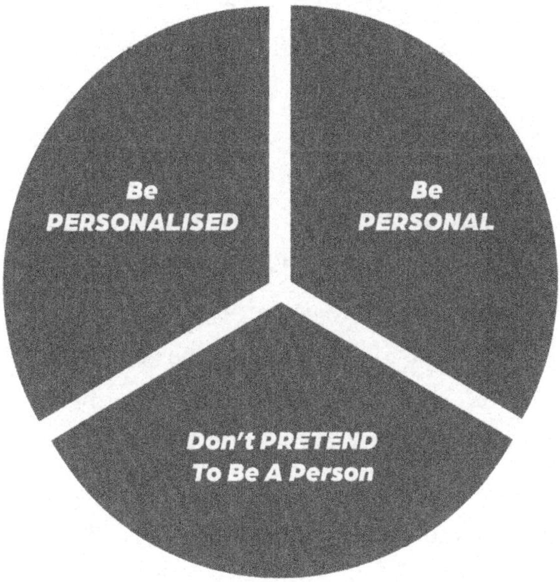

The 3 Ps of Automation

1. Be Personal

Some automation is generally better than no automation, but the more personal you can be the better. This falls into two categories: the content that is being sent to the prospect being more personal and service-orientated, and the segmentation of your audience being more personal based on the prospects' behaviours.

To illustrate this best, we have the speaker follow-up process from conferences and exhibitions that, when done well, can generate conversations with nearly everyone in the room after the event.

Step 1: Get Data!
For those who have done a lot of conferences, you will know that they are generally quite exhausting days, where delegates are speaking to a lot of other people, interacting with a lot of exhibitors and absorbing information from a variety of keynote speakers.

It should be a priority on the day simply to generate leads and collect data from potential prospects, and as a bonus, hope to get them booked in for a sales call. This doesn't mean just standing there to hand out business cards; this means speaking to prospects as often as you can, and if you feel you can help them, getting their data.

To make it easy for a prospect on the day, a great way to collect that data is by getting them to scan a QR code that simply asks for basic information to allow you to follow them up, and run through a fun demo of what you do. If you don't have a demo, those could be collecting data to provide them with a valuable resource, or even a competition (providing you make the competition prize relevant and interesting to your potential customers and not just a generic "win an iPad!" competition that will get anyone entering). This form completion is the simple trigger for the detailed follow-up that happens over the coming days.

The first thing that should be sent to them after they have finished speaking to you is usually a video later that night, at a time that the conference will have wrapped up, because you know they will ignore their phones during the day. After all, it is behaviourally natural for them to do so.

That video can be a WhatsApp video, and should simply thank them for speaking to you earlier and let them know what the next steps could look like. It is personal, and all about service, explaining that you know they will be tired and that the day will have been exhausting if they did it properly. Furthermore, it is personal because they will have seen you speaking, and will clearly have an expectation that you will be the one who will reach out later.

Step 2: Segmentation!

There are various ways at those conferences your prospects may see or speak to you. The main ways are seeing you presenting/speaking; at your stand as a delegate; at the stand as another exhibitor; around the venue speaking to a prospect; or finally if your prospect picks up a brochure from the stand when no one is looking.

Each of those options can have a different QR code and form, which, albeit looking the same to the end user, triggers a different set of automations. The actual video they can receive is based on the channel they came through, and while the actual skeletal structure is the same, the content is personal to how they interacted in the first place.

If they saw your presentation, the video triggered could thank them for watching and references things you would have spoken about in the talk. If they saw you at the stand, whether as a delegate or another exhibitor, the video could thank them for coming to the stand, and wish that they got enough out of the day as either a delegate or exhibitor. The brochure follow-up could be scanned at any time after the conference, so the videos are not time-specific, but should follow the same structure.

All of the videos that are sent out should be designed to be personal based on what the end user did, and the more personal it is by being related to what their day would have entailed, the more likely they are to respond.

Importantly, all of them state that the message is completely automated, and the expectations are set while they are inputting their data at the start, so it will always be received in the right way.

This is a great way of going from the 80 to the 90 on your 0-99 journey, as the core follow-up structure will automatically separate you from the crowd at those conferences, as not many businesses do this well at all – that is the 0-80. The specific videos for the particular QR code they scanned based on what piqued their interest or what they said to you on the day will take them from 80 to 90.

Step 3: Go Further If You Must!

This step will take you above the 90 mark, and it is having your follow-up be event-specific, and record a new set of those automations before every specific event. Everything in steps 1 and 2 can be done once and be applied to any conference by simply replacing the part where you would say, "Thank you for seeing me at XYZ event this weekend! How great was it seeing this specific speaker?" with "Thank you for seeing me at the conference this weekend, it was certainly one to remember!"

The skeletal structure or flow of the follow-up could be the same, but the content of the messages could be event-specific. This would hit home and be incredibly personal for the person receiving it, but would the extra effort of recording each video and replacing the new videos for the old each time you have an event booked really increase the sales opportunities? That's a judgement call for you to make.

2. Be Personalised

There is a fine line between being personalised and pretending to be a person, but when done correctly it can be incredibly effective.

One thing that is worth mentioning, is you can make the message as personalised as possible, but there comes a point where the time put into making each one personalised might as well be manual, which somewhat defeats the point.

The automated messages you are sending can pull through information that has been given to you by the prospect, and either include that information in outbound messaging (for example, First Name, Company Name, etc), or it can be used to filter what is sent to them. You may have different categories that your prospects fall into, and you can use their indications/choices/answers to questions you have asked them to complete to funnel them into the appropriate categories, which in turn sends them different material.

This is particularly important when it comes to qualifying people in and out, which we will cover in a Chapter later in the book, but the idea is that we offer the prospects the ability to indicate to your business whether they would or wouldn't be a good fit, and save time working that out later down the line.

Understanding that your prospects don't care about your business is, of course, important when it comes to what you are putting in the automations. Being personalised with what is being sent to them is a great way for them to begin to trust in you, and start the process of getting them to look past the fact that they don't care, and to see what you do as something that could benefit them.

It is a lot more effective to send a message that says, "Hi [first name]" instead of just "Hey," and have sentences in your messages that say, "Thank you for taking the time to speak to us about [your business] today", instead of "Thanks for your time earlier." We react better when things are more personalised and are also more likely to maintain that trust.

That isn't to say your prospects will think that you have manually sent it. But little touches do make a difference and make your prospects feel heard – something they will always yearn for.

3. Don't Pretend To Be Real

This is perhaps the biggest thing people get wrong when it comes to automation. They use it to try and replace what they would normally do. And in turn, they offer a worse experience for your prospect.

If you've ever interacted with some form of automation and got frustrated, whether it is copy-and-paste style replies or a website chatbot that says it is live but is actually AI, you will know how quickly someone's trust in automation falls.

A mistake a lot of business owners make is forcing people through a series of automation steps without adding any human element to make it easier for the business. But they forget their prospects' perspectives. Making things easier for you as a business – at the expense of the user experience – will rarely end well.

My father told me a story about a large supplier he worked with before he retired. He is an inspiration to me, from seeing his work ethic growing up to how much he has been there for me when I needed it most. He is also a very smart man, who understands the bigger picture when decisions are being made, which leads to him being the general manager of the company he worked for before he finished.

The supplier he told me about mandated all of their customers change the invoice method from what they had previously done to Direct Debits, around the time Direct Debits were being introduced into the banking system. It would have made it easier for them as a supplier, as payments would be more regular and late payments would be minimised.

The issue was, that wasn't how most businesses at the time operated. They were asking the businesses they worked with to change their fundamental behaviour and had assumed that they cared enough to change, and when they took a hard line, they lost a lot of business. Six months later, they came back with more flexible payment terms in a bid to get the business, but most suppliers had moved on and were working closer with their competitors. Shortly after that, they went under.

They were attempting to use automation at the expense of the human experience, and therein lies a problem. They saw the process and wanted to remove the human element of their accounting teams to save time, which nowadays would be a sensible choice. But at the time Direct Debits were so new it wouldn't have saved time, it would just pass the time burden onto the companies that frankly were paying their wages.

It isn't too difficult to set up an automation that looks as if it has been manually sent. This *can* initially have a great impact, and in isolation can boost a customer experience. The issue comes when that end user realises that they aren't actually engaging with a real person, and at that stage, the damage done to the trust they have built with the business can sometimes be irreparable.

If you have ever had a moment in a cinema where someone has broken your concentration by making too much noise, going on their phone or walking past to go to the toilet multiple times, you will know how that connection being broken can have a detrimental impact on the overall experience. Cinemas are immersive places, a chance to completely switch off from the world in a completely acceptable way, with a screen the size of a building, surround sound speaker systems, and sometimes, even more immersive 3D/4D offerings. Switching from immersion to distraction is sometimes at the speed of light, and that can happen to your users when they encounter something that isn't in line with what you are representing.

Combining the realisation by a prospect that you weren't a real person, with the user still at a stage where they don't care about you, any negative element of their experience will trigger an almost automatic end to the relationship. Pretending to be a human in the process will be seen as a lie, and bring into question everything else they could believe about your business. "If they lie about being a real person, what else are they lying about?"

You are Speaking to Humans

The journey your prospects go through will always be experienced by a human. And yet, many times businesses would overlook that fairly obvious fact.

Moreover, it will be experienced almost exclusively by humans who don't know the business as well as you do. Putting things in place that are personalised, personal and not pretending to be a person will be able to take those prospects through the small steps they need to get them to where you want them to be.

To do this, you need to take some time to plan that journey out from the ground up.

Thankfully, I've dedicated a Chapter to that. You're welcome.

Chapter 9
Failure To Plan Is Planning To Fail

This isn't a piece of advice that will be unique to this book – far from it in fact.

However, it is important to note that when you are thinking about what your prospects experience, they are likely going to be thinking differently to you, as we have discussed already. As a result, trying to get the experience looking and feeling good for the prospect is much harder without planning; off-the-cuff style suggestions and implementations are almost always driven by your perspective and rarely stop to think about the importance of your prospects' perspectives. This Chapter aims to structure that plan as best as possible and give you the tools to start implementing what has been learned so far.

This is particularly important for those who struggle to visualise the full process from start to finish, and those who have a more detailed customer journey than simply "click here to buy." It will form a foundational blueprint that you can always come back to and edit when needed, but will also allow you to have a training resource that your team can come back to whenever needed, making it easy for you to continue to implement those plans.

By having everything planned out, the time taken to build the customer journey from start to finish becomes more of a paint-by-numbers exercise. You will be able to see any parts of the process that could fall and plan for them. You will be able to come back to the laid-out plan and improve it as you learn more about your prospects. You will be able to use your plans as foundations for future new projects and journeys. All these things will benefit the business because it will benefit your customer experience.

Planning for what your prospects experience will have to be a balance between covering as many different personality profiles as possible, as well as being as personal as it could be for each. Some people will require more information and have all their questions answered, so having the answers to as many questions at hand would benefit them. However, for those who simply need to get to the point of buying, all of the information overload would actively put them off. There needs to be a process that covers those who need it to be as informative as possible, while also speeding it up for those who are ready to buy.

A good way to do this in this example is to have the FAQs easily accessible but not mandatory to read, so those who need the extra information can get it, and those who would be put off by information overload can look past it.

The best way to begin the process of planning is to disregard all the different ways someone could come in contact with the business. Thinking about every possible way someone could enquire, and every possible thing you want to send to each of those will frankly be overwhelming.

For example, let's take a business that may have six marketing verticals, with leads coming from organic social media, Google ads, referrals, inbound phone calls, paid social media ads and finally lead magnet downloads. If a standard customer journey currently has 10 touch points, including emails, messages, forms etc., that is automatically 60 things you need to plan out and organise.

Now, I could write something inspirational here about how you can set aside that time and completely overhaul what you are doing in one big shot, and there are some for whom that makes sense. However, for most in my experience, having that many tasks is a much harder undertaking and to even begin it would be difficult. And as you know, if things aren't easy, they are often forgotten about.

I feel sometimes that the advice given to business owners across the world is based on a utopian best-case scenario, and often it is not a practical way of running a business, at least initially.

"Hire staff and find the perfect person for that role and you will grow" completely forgets that staff costs money and that good people aren't easy to find.

The saying "There are 24 hours in a day, you can live on four hours of sleep and work the rest" is just stupid.

Once you get used to putting things in place and planning for new customer journeys, this will be like second nature. But when you are starting it is important to get something up and running. Done beats perfect every single time.

I mentioned previously about working towards 80, and the way to get there is to have a more generalised plan. Once that plan is created, you can look at the 80+ improvements by segmenting out your journeys. But for now, let's look at the core of what you are doing. Improve that, reach the 80, then move forward.

A lot of business owners struggle to get the 80 into practice because they are too focused on the 80-99, and as a result, the task of planning their customer journey becomes too daunting. The act of planning out the process, whether from a simple pen and paper or detailed documentation, aligns your strategy accordingly.

The result from doing so is not only a plan that is easier to create and, therefore easier to undertake in the first place, but also a blueprint you can come back to later that allows you to see where changes need to be made over time.

For the business in the example with six verticals, the 0 to 80 step is to have one general flow that everyone goes through. It may not be vertical-specific, but it is a hell of a lot better than not having anything across all verticals. The 80 to 90 step is to duplicate that over to the individual verticals, but we can't get there before we do the 0 to 80.

The best way to approach the plan is to think about the average prospect, while also planning for the worst-case scenario.

For clarity, there will always be outliers that simply you can't legislate for entirely. But at those points, you want to make it easy for a prospect to communicate with an actual human. People buy from people, so the process should be optimised to allow a human to jump in wherever needed, and encourage the prospect to ask questions where possible.

When planning out, simpler is better. There are lots of fancy tools out there to allow you to visualise each step, but I am still yet to find a tool that beats either a pen and paper or a whiteboard to draw out the steps.

As these steps need to be granular, it isn't as simple as saying, "They enquire, we want them to buy," so throughout this Chapter I want you to ask yourself the following:

What is the Easiest Way to Get a Prospect to Do the Next Thing?

As I've pointed out before, your prospects will need to have everything made easy for them. By viewing your planning from the perspective of someone not caring about the business, you will plan for eventualities that someone who is already prepared to buy from you wouldn't think, and therefore we have a more effective journey for everyone.

Crucially, what is easy for someone who cares about you is completely different to what is easy for someone who doesn't. The best bit about approaching from this perspective is by planning for someone who doesn't care, you make it incredibly simple for those who already do.

To do this, the best and most effective way is to approach your plan similar to how the channel tunnel was built. In the late 1980s, the channel tunnel construction began, with different tunnel boring machines starting on both the French and UK sides of the English Channel, with a view to finally connecting the two countries by rail. It was widely regarded as one of the most impressive and ambitious engineering projects of the time, and planning was of course essential.

Instead of focusing all their efforts in one direction from one side of the water, they began on both sides. Working out the start and end of the tunnels (depending on your perspective) with an aim of them meeting in the middle was always going to be the best and most efficient way of operating.

For the purposes of this plan, you have to work backwards first, then the last few steps will work in the right order.

Step 1: Get Them to Give You Money!
One thing most businesses are quite poor at planning is the part where someone gives you money. *This is the most important thing to get right.* Assuming you aren't running a charity, your business relies on getting customers to give you money. Even if you are a charity, that process needs to be easy. If you make it difficult for someone to give you money, you will struggle to generate revenue.

We previously talked about the story of a Mexican water seller who showed the importance of making it easy for customers. The example given of it being difficult was if they only provided the water in a can. An equally effective way of dissuading custom would be to make everything else easy, but only accept payment via a bank transfer to an exclusive Cayman Island bank in Bitcoin, which requires fast internet and a unique security process. The value gained versus the effort put in just isn't there. "Yes I cure my thirst, but what the fuck is a Bitcoin?"

There is a limit of course, but you should give your customers the facility to pay you in as many ways possible. Getting money is the most important part and should be the first thing you plan. Then you work backwards: How do they get to the payment page?

Step 2: Give Them More Options!

Once you know how someone is going to pay you, the next steps are fairly straightforward.

Take an incredibly effective process for high-ticket items that a client has implemented. This client offers sales training, and having a smooth process is incredibly important because if they can't get someone to buy, they aren't going to be great at training people in sales.

They take payments for what they do in either one-off upfront fees or payment plans with a deposit option. It's made easy for people looking for the best price or people looking to aid with cash flow forecasts. For either option, customers can pay by card, bank transfer, online money exchange services and any other sensible way to transfer money. An important realisation was the following: What is easiest for the business to receive payments isn't always the easiest for their clients. And what is easiest for their clients, brings them more money – that flip in mindset is a huge factor in increasing revenue.

Even at the point of paying you, your prospect doesn't care about you enough to go out of their way to give you money, so this step should be easy.

"We want the best price!" Great, there is an option for that.

"We want to spread the cost for cashflow reasons!" Great, there is an option for that.

"We want to pay a deposit and maybe clear the balance earlier!" Great, there is an option for that.

Saying this loud for people in the back: *If someone wants to give you money, let them.* As long as they are a values match and you can help them, let them give you money. Give them an option that suits you, and planning in advance for those options makes you sound confident when it comes to it.

Step 3: Sign on the Dotted Line...

Once the client knows that step, they know they also have to get a contract signed. They utilise a proposal system that allows prospects to be sent the proposal on their initial sales call, details the payment options and packages, acts as a contract that is signed and re-directs to the chosen payment page that either has instructions on how to pay via bank transfer or can accept card payments. This way, when a prospect says they are ready to work together, the steps for them to take are really simple and readily available to them.

Step 4: Deliver the Proposal.

Now that the process is in place, and you know that you will be sending that proposal to them on the initial sales calls, you have two things you need to solve: getting a prospect to the point where they are ready to sign that proposal, and how to have more calls where you create and send those proposals.

The easiest way is to book a follow-up call with the prospect when on the initial sales call with you and your business, that way there is a set time and date when you would speak again instead of it being left open-ended. If you needed to move that meeting it would be easier to do that than to just say, "I'll be in touch soon".

This is often a forgotten step but an incredibly important part of the sales process. Sending a prospect the information they need to sign up and then assuming they will just do so off their own back is naive. They still don't give a shit about you! The standard default for businesses is sending a proposal and then reaching out again in the future at a time that suits them, not the prospect. But booking a follow-up call with the prospect at the time that they are free is a natural next step and frankly should be the standard.

Step 5: Make Sure They Actually Turn Up!

The next step is making sure people turn up to that initial sales call (although this step could also apply to them turning up to that follow-up call). Plan out a reminder series of messages that initially confirm the details at the point of booking, then remind the prospect of the call seven days, 24 hours and one hour before the call is due to start. The contents of those messages should be more than just simple reminders, but videos that encourage questions to be asked in the build-up to the call set expectations and lay out clearly what would happen if they are ready to proceed.

The individual elements in this step are laid out in more depth in the next Chapter because most businesses skip the step of lowering the number of no-shows in their sales process. They just assume there will be a certain amount of no-shows, so they don't try and fix it.

To see my full customer journey plan from start to finish, just send me the word **PLAN** on WhatsApp.

After those five steps are completed, the next step is to get more sales calls booked in, and the next Chapter will detail what those processes look like.

After you have planned out the structure of these steps, the important part is the content of what was being sent out from an email and WhatsApp perspective. Writing and recording those messages is the next stage in the process, as they need to be created before the structure is fully built out, but not before the structure is planned. The plan gives you a list of the content you need to create, and that list is a lot easier to tackle when you have it all in front of you instead of making it on the fly when you can.

By designing and planning, you are creating a journey that is the default someone will experience, and the foundation upon which everyone will start. The fast movers in your sales pipeline will have the opportunity to skip steps and fast-track themselves, while the analytical buyers will be shown how to have that information presented to them which will help them all get to the same place.

The clarity in this planning also helps the actual human in the process – either the salesperson or you as a business owner – because when speaking to your prospects you can be confident in the knowledge that when they do the next step, certain things will happen. That confidence will shine through to prospects, and we will detail that more later in the book.

Once you have the core framework of this plan written down, make sure it is safely documented somewhere. This Chapter started by stating that writing the framework plan is much more effective than any fancy tools that visually allow you to plan out the process. For this stage in the process, that is correct. However, once you are at the point where the framework has been planned and designed, then it is worth using some of those tools so you have a resource you can always go back to when needed later on. These can be as simple as creating a PDF document that anyone in your team can access, or fancy flow-building tools, depending on your level of expertise and how pretty you like things to look.

One bit of bad news I will break to you here is that when you start automating and designing your processes in detail like this, you will want to tweak and change that process as time goes on. The way to balance that is to set some time aside every few months to reevaluate what the process looks like and overhaul the big parts if you feel it necessary. Between those days set aside, you can add small changes, but note what changes you are making and add them to that resource you created as a PDF or fancy flow.

Over time, automations overlap very quickly. Human behaviour has no end to the possible outcomes, despite generally being predictable. But the more possibilities you plan for, the more places your process can fall if you aren't carefully noting the steps. This is the extra effort you will jump off from after you have done the 0-80 steps and are attempting to go past 80+.

One final, often overlooked step in planning what happens is adding exclusions and removal steps in your automation. Once someone in your process acts on the next step you have designed, having automations that ask them to complete that step would be the opposite of good service, and just annoying. For example, if part of your process is to get a sales call booked in, having them prompted to book that call after the call has been booked can have a negative impact.

By planning these steps out, everything becomes incredibly easier in implementation. You can effectively visualise your customers going from one stage to another, what options they have, variants you want them to go through, qualification steps, and where everyone will end up. When there is no dead end for your prospect, there is somewhere for them to go. That may be qualified out, it may be in a free community, or it may well be them sending you money. The latter is the aim and is a lot easier when you have planned for it.

Chapter 10
Expectations & Next Steps

I'd go as far as to say the biggest frustration people have when interacting with businesses is usually rooted in a misalignment of expectations on one side. Without sugarcoating things, it is 100% your job as the business to set that expectation.

If someone tells you they will arrive at a certain time and they are late, the frustration is down to misaligned expectations. If you order a taxi straight away and it takes 20 minutes, the issue is again, misaligned expectations.

Mastering this Chapter in everything you do with a prospect – from your automations to your in-person, marketing and internal conversations – will have the biggest impact on your prospect's experience, and therefore the largest increase in conversion rates going through your sales process.

If you are confused and frustrated at a prospect failing to do the thing you expected them to do, this Chapter will help solve a lot of those issues.

As consumers, we have certain expectations that have been built over decades of buying behaviour. A great example of this was laid out amazingly by the very impressive Rymel Dmot when talking about buying a car.

The example is as follows: Imagine someone comes up to you randomly and offers you a brand new, top-of-the-range Ford Focus car, no strings attached, and the price is £100. For context, that is a car that typically would be worth £29,000 to £42,000 brand new.

There is pretty much no one in the world who would look at that deal and not hesitate while thinking, "Right, what's the catch?"

In reality though, that would be the deal of a lifetime on paper for a lot of people. There is nothing negative about the offer, it is all positive. But society in general knows that if it sounds too good to be true, it probably is. Our expectations have been formed even subconsciously by things around us – past experiences, societal norms, previously negative/positive customer journeys, family and friend influences and more – that we simply don't notice.

What's funnier about the reaction is that the person selling the car knows this is the deal of the century, and cannot fathom why no one is snapping up the deal. "Is it still too expensive?"

What Rymel's example clearly demonstrates is how a business owner might see an offer as amazing from their perspective, but fail to consider the views of people who don't care or trust them. In his example, most of the questions are negative, which oddly enough, makes it harder to build trust as you start on the back foot.

Your expectations as a business owner and the expectations of the person experiencing your business for the first time will almost always be different. You are an expert in what you do, you know more about it than most people. You don't generally start a business without knowing a good amount more than your customers.

Your prospects don't care enough about what you do yet, because if they did, the chances are they would have been customers already.

You therefore need to be incredibly clear on what the expectations should be for your prospect, and whether you do that manually or through automation, it is still a vital part of their experience.

You can mitigate almost any element of a negative experience by being clear with expectations and communication. Too often businesses are hesitant to deliver something that sets expectations for fear of their prospects reacting negatively, but the lack of communication and expectations has the opposite impact.

There is a point to be made about underpromising and overdelivering, so there are some things that can be held back. If you send over a welcome gift when clients come on board, for example, you don't need to tell them in advance that it is coming. Being surprised is a good thing.

No One has Ever Been Disappointed by Their Expectations Being Exceeded

And here is the great news: It is you as the business owner who sets the expectations for your prospects. Remember, they don't care about you, so they definitely don't have any expectations. That's your job.

I'll say that bit again: *You set your prospect's expectations.*

If you fail to do that in the process your prospects go through, they will start to set their own expectations. The chances of those being correct are slim to none because they don't know enough about you yet. Taking chances on what your prospects' expectations are at this stage is problematic, to say the least.

The second bit of great news is that it is very easy to do, as long as you plan well, consider your prospect's perspective, remember they don't care, and do so as quickly as possible, ideally through automation.

Previously, you learned about first impressions and the example of a restaurant that had a delay in food. The problem was solved when the delay was explained immediately – the waiter set the expectations clearly.

Those expectations are completely in your control to set and should be done at every possible stage of the process, plus having them reinforced at each contact point.

To be clear, setting your prospect's expectations should also be combined with you at least meeting those expectations, if not exceeding them. That's on you, and something you have to deliver on.

If you typically can call a prospect within 48 hours of their enquiry with a maximum of 72 hours, you should set the expectation that someone will be in touch within 72 hours. When you call within 48 hours, you are already impressing them.

If what you produce is usually delivered within a week, you tell your customers that delivery is usually within seven to 10 days, often faster. When it gets delivered five days later, you are already impressing them.

If what you offer is a service that requires a lot of input on the customer's part, you need to set that expectation before they buy; otherwise, you just have the headache later down the line. When they actually end up doing less work because you have over-delivered, you are actively impressing them.

This is a particularly difficult fact to accept for people pleasers who want to do everything they can to avoid a conflict.

I worked with a great man in Mallorca while working on boat parties. He was a fantastic person, but he couldn't deal with conflict and said yes to a lot of things that conflicted with others.

One day, we had a boat that was sold out, and we had a rule that guests had to arrive at 2:15pm at the latest. After that point, if we had space, we filled that space with people that were on a waiting list. Being Mallorca, we often had people not turning up to the boats after a long session the night before, and that rule allowed us to always have a full boat.

The numbers on the boat were strict, as the capacity of the boat was a licensed requirement to sail. I remember it to this day: 145 guests plus the boat's crew, of which, 138 were paying guests, and the rest were reps who worked with us.

On this day, we had reached that number. I then had a group of four that turned up late and couldn't get onto the boat. Understandably they weren't the happiest, but again we reminded them of the expectations on their part that they had to turn up at 2:15pm, and the time they arrived was 2:35pm. The issue was solved quickly as we moved them to the boat the following day, guaranteed they would be first on the boat, got them a free drink at the bar and that was that. They weren't ecstatic but as we had set expectations, they knew it was their fault. And we knew that the following day they would forget all about it because of the quality of the experience we delivered.

When the people pleaser I worked with turned up, he went around and happened upon the group of four, who relayed that they were gutted they weren't on the boat.

Again, I stress that the issue has already been sorted at this stage. However, not being one to deal very well with conflict, he went behind the desk when no one was there, grabbed four wristbands and told them, "It will be fine." They were happy, he was happy.

Fast forward 10 minutes, and everyone gets up and leaves for the boat. They got up with everyone else and got on the boat with the rest of the crowd. As everyone boarded, the numbers being counted on by the crew kept going up. 136… 137… 138.

That was capacity, and the last four people, who *weren't* in that group, were told they couldn't board. Four random people who had done everything correctly and all of a sudden were told that their plans were cancelled and they had no choice. The boat left, with those four on the pier, and my colleague who caused the issue in the first place to deal with a bigger problem.

The point of the story is that problems can be mitigated with good communication and clear expectations to fall back on. Being the people pleaser in the situation causes more problems than it solves, and that scenario created four very angry customers who demanded a full refund, and no doubt told everyone around the pool the following day about how bad the experience had been. All completely unnecessary

When a prospect interacts with your business, it should lay out what the expectations are, and the best way to do that is to clearly define the next steps.

What *Are* Your Next Steps?

Think of your customer journey as a staircase, with the first floor being them enquiring and the second floor being the next stage of the process (in this example we will call it a discovery call). There are people who will struggle up those stairs, some who will jump three steps at a time, and others who will find a lift to get to the next floor with the minimum amount of effort.

But importantly, if you don't provide a staircase with multiple touchpoints, they are unlikely to get upstairs. Also, once someone gets three-quarters of the way up the staircase, the chances of them getting to the end are much higher.

These micro touch points don't just get someone from one small step to the next; they build trust with the business at each stage. Setting smaller expectations chronologically as they get from one touch point to another starts to build a reputation for delivering on what you promise.

When you are planning, you need to work out what those next steps look like – in as much detail as possible.

Previous Chapters have focused on planning and making things easy; below will be how to optimise from the initial lead process to getting someone to book a call in. In the last Chapter, Step 5 focused on getting those leads to book in sales calls; here we detail that more.

Leads coming into the business for the first time are at their peak interest, yet also at the point where their interest could diminish if they are going to buy. Therefore, they need touchpoints.

Your leads should immediately get a message, preferably a video, that thanks them, builds trust by being more personal and sets clear expectations that the next step is to book a call or have you call them.

When creating the video it should state at the beginning that later on you will have answered some of the most common questions you get asked (which covers those that need more information), have a link to your services (which covers those that are just interested in the logistics and fees), and have a button for them to book a call (which covers those that are ready to book straight away).

Should a call not be booked, or the prospect specifically say they aren't interested, they should receive further videos and messages from you over a period of time that makes sense for your business, while being more persistent than you think as you learned previously.

The second video should be more personal, a bit about you, your business and what your values are, while the remaining videos cover success stories, offering to answer questions and being quite to the point about whether they are actually interested or not.

Each message should clearly communicate what their expectations should be, whether they respond or not. This ensures they are fully aware of the next steps and can make a well-informed decision.

Once a call is booked, send them a reminder message and a video 24 hours before the sales call. This should clearly outline what to expect during the call. It is transparent that they are having a sales call, with an aim to potentially do some business together, and lays out the structure of the call. It also explains clearly what the next steps would look like should business be done together, including letting them know that a proposal will be sent and what they would need to do to get it signed.

Importantly, at each stage of the process, you should be laying out expectations and next steps, and continue to meet or exceed those expectations at every turn. If you state you will call someone within 24 working hours, that should be less, and ideally, as soon as you possibly can. In the event you can't meet those expectations, you should communicate well enough to realign those expectations if possible.

For example, if you are running late on delivering a project that isn't great. You can either communicate with your customer and say, "Hi [customer name], I wanted to send a message to let you know that we are running late on delivering the project due to [reason]. Obviously, we are disappointed and are sorry, and I wanted to let you know it will be done by [x date] and is our top priority," which has a chance of being received well the earlier it is sent. Or, if you don't send anything and it's late, then you are making excuses and looking unprofessional.

A Lot Can be Achieved by Having Aligned Expectations

Each of the steps you should look at putting into place needs to be easy, logical and progressive. The number of steps you should have will differ massively depending on the business you have, and, crucially, the appropriate time intervals between them. Typically high investments take a little longer, whilst lower ticket items can have shorter gaps between steps.

I rely heavily on automation for these steps, for reasons we will cover in the next few Chapters. But also because setting expectations is a lot easier when the expectations are the same for every lead going through the process.

This is where the value of that human connection comes in: You can state in your automation that the message being sent is automatic, but it is there to set expectations and let them know what happens next so that between the initial contact and the human contact, they aren't left feeling anxious.

Getting a prospect from their enquiry to buying from you is a big leap, you need a lot of things to go right for you in the process for that to happen. Getting someone to commit to smaller steps through the process is actually quite easy.

This is the core of where your conversion rates will grow because by looking at each step in micro detail, you can get more people to finish the process.

For example, if you convert 20% of the people that have a sales call with you, getting more people onto those calls in the first place will increase your revenue and tighten up the conversion rate from enquiry to call.

Furthermore, if you do it correctly and set expectations, the chances of that 20% increasing in the first place is high.

By having that core process planned out and enacted, you can have the consistency that allows you to scale, as well as the confidence when you are speaking to them in the human parts between the automation on what their experience both has been so far and will be moving forward.

A prospect who knows what is coming and is still coming along for the journey is a hell of a lot more likely to do the thing that is coming. If you were told when filling out an enquiry form that someone on a sales team would call you to book a meeting in, and you still filled it out already, will your reaction to that call be negative? Probably not.

The fear a lot of businesses have here is that being clear and open will diminish the number of people booking calls with their sales team, and they believe that their sales team will "convince" them to buy anyway. That simply leads to poorer quality calls, misaligned expectations when you go to deliver the actual offering you have, and overall a shit environment to be in, for lack of a better phrase.

Imagine going into sales calls where your prospects know what is coming, are excited about it, and know what needs to happen for them to buy.

Imagine your leads only coming into your team's call list specifically knowing those calls are coming.

Imagine a lead having expectations aligned with your business within minutes of enquiring because of a video it took you no time to send.

Now imagine that happening with every prospect you have. That is the power of setting clear expectations.

Chapter 11
Confidence In Consistency

In the 2008 Beijing Olympics, Usain Bolt blew the world away and quickly became one of the most exciting athletes anyone had ever seen. The Olympics are always a global spectacle, and these games were in part defined by Bolt finishing the 100m in a new world record time of 9.69s, beating his own world record set earlier that year.

They weren't Bolt's first Olympics; he debuted in 2004 running in the 200m and 400m, and was widely considered too tall for the 100m. In fact, he only started running the 100m competitively a year earlier: He struck a deal with his coaches that if he could run under 10.30s he would drop the 400m. He ran 10.03s in Crete and went on to break the world record in only his 5th competitive race at 9.72s, the record that was broken in Beijing.

A fact that makes my mind boggle is that in the weeks before that final race, Bolt consumed around 1,000 chicken nuggets, or approximately 100 a day.

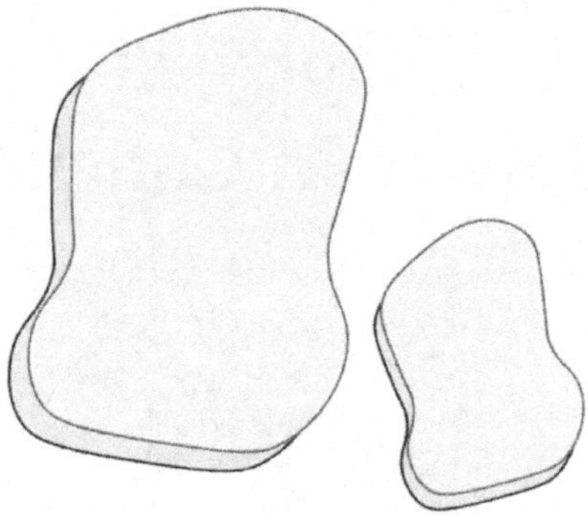

Not that I have a problem with chicken nuggets, we are actually good friends, but typically they aren't the first food that comes to mind when thinking about someone breaking a world record in one of the most watched events.

Why did he do it? Consistency.

Bolt talked in his book *The Fastest Man Alive*:

> "Honestly, I ate nothing else in all my time out in China except chicken nuggets. They were the only food I could properly trust, which wouldn't affect my stomach. On arriving at the [pre-Olympic] training

> camp I'd tried a local Chinese meal, which wasn't like the ones we eat in the West, and my body didn't react well. So, knowing I could rely on nuggets, I made up my mind that was all I would eat. And eat them I did, for breakfast, lunch and dinner, washed down with bottled water."

The biggest risk to him not performing in that race was being ill in the weeks before. He had done the hard work of perfecting what he does, so getting better in the weeks before the race wasn't going to make a difference. What would have made the difference is getting sick. One of the reasons McDonald's is the most popular restaurant in the world is that you can walk into one anywhere around the world and know what you are going to get. That consistency, combined with the ease of ordering and the speed, is the main reason it went from one restaurant to over 41,000 in 2024.

Bolt understood that the chances of him getting sick from chicken nuggets were very small, and that is because McDonald's can generally be relied on for food that won't get you sick. It's consistent, and that is important.

You Cannot Scale Rapidly Without Consistency and Systems

By understanding that consistency is incredibly important, you can start implementing systems designed to make everyone's journey through your customer process smooth and structured. Ideally, these systems should be optimised to move people seamlessly from one step to the next, as we learned in the last Chapter.

You want to be able to sit back and know that every prospect interacting with your business is having the same experience, intertwined with the personal nature of what you offer.

Why do the largest brands in the world that generally have front-facing staff usually have uniforms? Consistency in branding.

Why do most supermarket chains have set criteria for laying out their stores? Consistency in experience.

Why do road signs around the UK have the same font and sizing criteria? Consistency causes the safety of the signs to increase.

Why does the London Underground have the same style map everywhere? Consistency means people don't get as confused, meaning a more pleasurable experience.

Consistency gives your prospects a lot of clarity while also giving you peace of mind. If your prospects all go through the same process, you don't need to worry about them missing a bit of information they need or having the right expectations going into the next call.

When you travel through an airport, every stage of that process has been planned out meticulously. When you board a plane, the ground crew can confidently tell you what your experience was on arrival, through security, what you had to remove and place in the security bins, where you had to walk, what gate you went through, and what plan you got on. That needs to be consistent and clear for obvious safety reasons; so why can't that be the same for your business?

You should be in a position when you finally speak to a prospect to be able to say, "You saw this advert, filled in this form, have been sent this, read this, answered this and gave me this information. Because of that, I feel I can help, so let me ask you a few more questions."

That clarity in the process and the consistency allows you to sound confident on the call, and that confidence is something that builds trust with a prospect.

The flip side of that coin is sounding like you don't know what you are talking about. I ask this question again: When was the last time you gave money to someone you thought didn't know what they were talking about?

This confidence not only helps your prospects trust in you and start caring a little more about you, but it also brings you peace of mind that takes a lot of stress off your plate.

Your Mindset is Vital

Have you ever noticed how a lot of outspoken affluent people talk more about their state of mind than they do about anything else? It's because being in the right mindset plays an incredibly important part in their success.

If you've ever had a holiday, then come back from it and feel more energised than ever, it is because you need to have downtime, you need to relax and you need to be doing things to make sure you are in the right mindset. It isn't easy, and this book isn't your go-to book for mindset education. But if you are waking up every day in a poor state of mind, that is never going to be positive for your business.

Not a lot of this book has focused on your mindset in business, which has been a driving factor behind my own personal growth. Finding things that reduce the stresses in your own day-to-day is a vital part of success because you have to ask yourself this question: Is your business a success if you aren't happy?

That's a tough question to answer. It's often a hard realisation for a lot of people, whose biggest driving factor in their business is increasing profits. At the end of the process, profits mean money and people think money means happiness.

Spoiler alert: It doesn't.

It bloody well helps, it removes stresses that you would have otherwise. But if it is the only driving force behind your wanting to grow a business, it is a rocky path to fall down.

One of the core aims of this book is to give you back time to work on the business, not work solely within it.

Is working 16 hours a day to grow the business without taking a step back a successful outcome for you?

And perhaps a more blunt question: If you're working a lot now in hopes that a growing business will give you time back later, what do you have in place to ensure that happens?

Having consistent processes with automation, designed to build customer trust and show you care about them, makes it easy for them to engage and value their time. This can ultimately give you more of your own time back. You will be confident enough in the process that everyone is going through, so you can relax a little more. And because big portions of the process are being automated, you will have the time to put that more relaxed headspace into business growth.

Can You Currently Take a Holiday?

This was a tough question that I had to ask myself: Can I comfortably take time off from the business and allow my systems to take the brunt of the work?

It took time to get there, but having that confidence in what has been put in place has allowed me to spend more time away from working in the business.

I do this by implementing heavily structured weeks.

Mondays and Wednesdays are new sales conversation days. They are the only days I have sales calls and they are all I take on those days to allow me to get in the right mindset. Most of the time, those days are filled through automation without me needing to do any work at the front end. Tuesdays and Thursdays I have client meetings and block out time for client-orientated work, to allow me to deliver on the expectations I have already set. Fridays are personal days where I focus on my own personal growth, and don't take meetings unless they relate to that. I don't work the weekends, and I aim to have two to three holidays a year.

All this is due to having automation in place, ensuring consistency and clear expectations throughout the process.

Whilst there is effectiveness in that consistency, you do need to be both flexible and human to make everything work. As laid out in a previous Chapter, your leads are actual people who differ in how they deal with everything.

You don't have to sell to everyone, and you should only work with people who align with your values. I could write a whole other book on the joy that brings to you, but the core message is that by clearly laying out who you are and what you/your business stands for, you will qualify out the people who are not a joy to work with. We'll cover more of this in the next two Chapters.

Giving people options throughout the process to steer them in the direction that most suits their personalities is ultimately the best way to get your prospects through your processes. However, there comes a point where you need to have the human touch.

This comes back to the understanding that there is a limit to where automation ends and the human-to-human conversation begins.

Once you have the core consistency worked out, you can drop in and out of the process to answer questions where needed. The standard process that everyone will consistently go through is the skeletal framework that defines their journey and sets their expectations, with the human elements intertwined where needed.

They start the journey not caring about your business, but if at each point where they could abandon it, you have consistently exceeded expectations, you then start to remove barrier after barrier between them enquiring and them giving you money.

More conversations like that with time saved will scale the business, and bring you time back.

Most of what this process looks like is after the enquiry point; the next two Chapters will cover the inbound side of the equation.

Chapter 12
Open the Floodgates

Once you have mastered understanding your prospects – leaning into what is natural and easy – and have begun the process of automating those next steps, you can start attracting leads into the business at a much higher rate.

This Chapter will explore how combining everything that has been covered so far in the book, you can start scaling at a much higher rate. Many marketers will tell you to only deal with qualified leads and add steps to the process people go through, to ensure your time is only taken by conversations that are likely to be ready to buy. Whilst there is some merit in that, the advice is flawed.

In my opinion, once you have understood someone's behaviour and automated part of their customer journey, you can do a lot more work at the start of their experience to attract prospects earlier in the sales process. By using automation we can qualify those leads and direct them to the appropriate areas of your business without taking any extra time away from you – all while building a community of potential customers at a much faster rate.

That ability to consistently scale can be the foundation of a long-term successful business.

Why is it important to make it easier for people to join your community while bringing everything else together? There are many benefits, but the first of which is you are almost guaranteeing more customers.

Imagine two different campaigns, where the first is incredibly easy for someone to join the community, and the second one has put a few extra barriers up to only end up with qualified leads. If Campaign 1 generates 100 leads, and Campaign 2 generates 10 leads, many marketers will say that those 10 leads are better than the 100, because they are more qualified.

The logic does make sense, although I believe it is flawed. The 10 people who are happy to go through the extra steps in Campaign 2 would definitely go through the easy steps in Campaign 1.

The logic some marketers will tell you that makes Campaign 2 better is that you won't be able to work out who those 10 are out of the 100 if you simply get more people into the community. Therefore, there are a lot of wasted hours trying to qualify the right people.

The difference is that when you have a well-designed, behaviourally natural customer journey that has been built with the prospects in mind, and automated where it can and should be, you can get the 10 filtered very easily and potentially get others that are part of the remaining 90 through the process too.

Therefore the worst case scenario is that you still have the 10 that were interested in Campaign 2, plus the actual likelihood that you end up with more qualified leads.

By putting automated customer journeys in place, I have been able to increase the number of leads coming into the business tenfold, without there being any extra time allocated. That increase has resulted in a much steadier flow of work and a more consistent conversion rate. This consistency makes the business more successful in the longterm, and means that we can put plans in place to continue scaling, while having the time to actually implement them.

In order to achieve this, you need to understand this simple fact: If we offer more value to a prospect earlier in the process than the effort they have to put in, they will likely do the thing we want them to do.

When a prospect first interacts with the business, and they are at the stage where they don't care, it is unlikely you are going to get them to commit to something where you as a business receive more value than they do. That value exchange should be in favour of the prospect throughout the process, so we need to ask the question, "How do we provide more value at the early stages?

This can be done in a number of different ways, but should all have one thing in common: They encourage the prospect to feel like they are getting a bargain.

The earlier that happens in the process, the bigger the gap between a prospect's effort and the value they get.

I am going to give four detailed examples of how this can be implemented, and should only be done when the follow-up process after they move towards the business is built and is already robust.

Lead Magnets

These are some of the most common and indeed simple ways to get people to input their details and become part of your business community.

They can be simple PDF downloads that you have created, and which offer an education they would ordinarily not have. It is both a huge amount of value in exchange for just their details, while also positioning you as the expert in that particular field. By creating multiple lead magnets you can target different audiences, whilst also being able to bundle these together in an online resource that you could eventually sell for a monetary value.

By giving away these lead magnets for free as part of your front-end marketing, you can run a campaign whereby someone simply needs to fill in a form and agree to further contact in exchange for the resources.

If you are a marketing company looking for clients who need help with their social media marketing, you could offer a lead magnet called, "The 5 top tips for improving your social media marketing."

If you are a coach specialising in sales, looking for businesses that need to improve their sales, you could have a lead magnet called, "The common sales mistakes and how to fix them."

You can also get the top five things that your customers ask you about, and create a resource that answers those questions.

You will get people who just want the resource and will never work with the business, but those who are potential customers will download the resource, and see the quality that you offer while beginning to see you as the expert. This makes the level of trust they have in you increase. And by having an automated follow-up process that links to what they are likely to do anyway, you can comfortably get them from that initial step of downloading to the next step, which could be booking in a call with you as a business.

Webinars

These can often be a more specific lead magnet, but webinars are a great way of getting someone to not only indicate they are interested but also build that trust that you are the expert. Typically, these fall into three categories: immediate-access webinars, evergreen pre-recorded webinars and live-scheduled webinars.

There are pros and cons for each of course, but the logic is the same for all of them: If you can get someone to commit 30-60 minutes of their attention to you from the first point of contact by giving free value away, they will be much further down the sales process than if they simply were simply asked at the start to book a sales call with you.

These also allow the opportunity for you to inform them of the best ways to work together, so they would be speaking to you after the webinar with more of an understanding of what that could look like, which naturally makes them more likely to proceed.

Immediate-Access Webinars

With immediate-access webinars, you are giving someone the option to join a webinar that is starting imminently according to the time that they register their interest. This can reduce the rate of no-shows at events but does involve them committing a large amount of time immediately, where their interest would only have been spiked when they saw the advert moments before. It is an accelerated way of getting interest, which can be incredibly effective but is difficult to get those who can't commit the larger amount of time at that stage onto another event in the future.

Evergreen Pre-Recorded Webinars

Evergreen pre-recorded webinars are the least time-consuming for you as a business, as generally they are recorded once and then broadcast on repeat at set times during the week, with the leads registering for the replay time that suits them. Whilst I am not a great fan of pretending they are live, the idea that the prospect is watching the webinar with other people that could be live can be very effective.

Live-Scheduled Webinars

Live-scheduled webinars are generally some of the most effective approaches. They do require adding time to the calendar for each session, but when used well, they can convert into a regular stream of sales. People know they are live, and you can easily update them based on industry changes and your operations.

Regardless of the option, the value exchange for the webinar needs to be incredibly large for the prospect. This can be achieved by offering free or nominal-fee access to the webinar, with the potential for an upgraded experience that provides them with more resources and value for an additional fee.

During these webinars, there should be information on how to work with you and the business, along with a time-limited offer available exclusively until the webinar concludes, making it a compelling opportunity to sign up.

Staggered Events

A great strategy is to stagger events that offer more and more value, with financial commitments being added at each stage before the final high-end product. These could easily involve an intro event, which is either completely free or requires a deposit that is returned when they attend. The latter normally has fewer no-shows, while the former will have a higher rate of people registering but not turning up.

The secondary event could be a larger-scale event, either over an extended period of time or in a more exclusive group. But to attend this step there needs to be a larger financial commitment.

Following that event, there could be an introduction to the larger commitment or higher ticket item that you offer, whether that be a 1-to-1 or a more high-end offering.

At each stage of the staggered event process, there will be dropoffs similar to how people will abandon the sales process in any other business. However, the trust that prospects are developing with your business through the events is a lot higher.

Challenges

These are increasingly popular, focusing on a limited time frame where you can showcase a teaser of what you offer. It allows them to experience the value you bring when working together.

Typically these challenges would involve larger groups, and over a small period of time, like three days or five days. Free challenges would bring in a large amount of people, while paid challenges can involve smaller groups. However, like all the other options, the value exchange is heavily in favour of the prospect.

For example, if you run a PR agency, your 5-day challenge could be "How to get published in your ideal magazines," attracting people inherently interested in magazine publication—ideal prospects for your business.

With the last three of these options, there would need to be a dedicated follow-up series that covers the lead from the initial registration stage to turning up at the event. This is because the show-up rate will have a direct impact on how many people move on to the step that follows on from the event.

All of these options can open the floodgates to leads coming into the business. They offer choices that, for the most part, don't require extra time from your business to implement but attract prospects to start engaging with your community and building trust with the business.

Combining these strategies with advertising across any traditional medium—whether print advertising, social media, paid ads, search engine optimisation, or even media advertising like radio or TV—you can attract a wider network of people into the top end of the business.

You can then funnel them through these strategies combined with a customer journey designed to maximise your chances of moving prospects from one step to the next.

Whether getting someone to sign up for a webinar, download a lead magnet, attend a series of events or a challenge, you need to make that process as easy as possible and make it clear what the steps in the build-up to the event and following on after the event actually look like.

There is kindness in clarity, and being clear that people who would be downloading or signing up would also be the ideal customer for the business is incredibly important. There is no point in running a webinar on "the importance of HR within business" if your business doesn't have anything to do with HR.

The biggest part of this strategy that will impact your business falls into two categories: First, you can scale consistently when you have a steady stream of leads coming into the business, all of which indicate they would be interested in what you offer. Second, the larger your interested community becomes the more options you have moving forward with regards to marketing strategies.

When creating these strategies, ask yourself this: Would my ideal customer be interested in this offering? If the answer is anything other than a resounding yes, it isn't something worth spending time developing. If the answer is unequivocally positive, then you have built a list of people who have already indicated that they are interested in what you have to offer.

That list is one of the most valuable things you will have, as you own the list yourself and can advertise back to them whenever you need. The next Chapter will cover qualifying those people and making sure the quality of that list is maintained.

Chapter 13
QPR

It took me 13 Chapters to bring the acronym QPR into the book, and I have absolutely no regrets at all!

Regardless of the cleverly concealed football reference, this Chapter is one of the most important ones and is partly so because it helps you manage your inbound prospects in order of priority. But it is mainly important because of how it massively helps your mindset, and frankly your mental health.

This Chapter will focus on what happens after you open the floodgates to the leads coming into the business, and the importance of qualifying those leads, keeping your database fresh and full of actively interested prospects. We will also discuss why offering people the option to tell you they aren't the right fit is in everyone's best interest.

Once more people are brought into the business, it can escalate quickly. This is a good problem to have; more leads mean more potential sales, right? If it isn't managed correctly it can quickly get out of control and the quality of the database will start to decrease. That quality has an impact, and we will explore why that is the case further in this Chapter.

What is QPR?

Qualification
Purification
Rejection

QPR stands for: **Q**ualification, **P**urification, and **R**ejection.

Qualification plays a big role here because we need to make sure the leads are being effectively qualified through your business processes. This covers a lot of different things, but the best way I like to see it is using your process the same way an air traffic controller directs planes. Each one is valuable but needs clear and specific directions. Some planes do exactly the same journey, some are vastly different.

Purifying your database means keeping that quality consistent over time by removing people who no longer fit what you're looking for—whether they no longer align with your values, their priorities have changed, or they no longer have the problem you solve.

Rejection is not only allowing you to be rejected by your prospects, but it is also actively encouraging them to do so when it isn't a good fit for them. Not only can this build trust with you as a business, but it also takes the pressure off, and we will touch on that in more depth as we continue.

Doing these three things well is so important when it comes to both the quality of your prospect's experience, but also your own experience interacting with them. Most of this book has been rightly focusing on thinking about things from your prospect's point of view, but for a brief moment in this Chapter, I want to focus on the impact of having great conversations with people who have enjoyed their experience so far.

Our own mental health is incredibly important when it comes to running a business, something that I have personally struggled with. There are things I have put in place which have impacted my mindset when it comes to my business (and by extension, my entire life), and I want to share them in this part.

In late 2022, I travelled to Austin, Texas on a business trip that I was really looking forward to. For a variety of reasons, I was looking forward to having a break, and looking back now I know it was because of the stress I was under. I also didn't realise at the time how it was the beginning of seeing things differently from my previous business partner, someone I consider a dear friend of mine.

We flew with Virgin Atlantic, and took advantage of their "bid for an upgrade" option, where we could place a bid for an automatic upgrade to first class should there be any space available. To our fortune, the flights were upgraded a few days before we were due to board.

I made a few pivotal mistakes before the trip though. Firstly I built my hopes up that this trip could be the break I desperately needed. Secondly, I tried to organise a few business meet-ups in the city before arriving, but I didn't put enough effort into ensuring their success, and frankly, they flopped.

At the time, I didn't realise the desperation with which I needed this break. A break that didn't come.

Austin is a great city, and there are some things that were amazing about the trip. My very first transatlantic flight was truly an amazing first-class experience.

Steve Harvey, a very popular comedian, host and motivational speaker from the USA once said, "Pay a little extra and fly first class. Once you get in first class, you see how wide the seats are, everybody gets a washcloth, they've got a menu where you get to decide what you want, and all the drinks are free. Once you sit in first class, the next time you get on a plane, it's very difficult to walk past those seats, and then your mind starts thinking of ways to get back to first class. And guess what, that's what you start attracting to your life and you start behaving and producing stuff to get you back into first class."

As we entered Heathrow Airport through a private entrance reserved for first-class guests, with our bags taken from the car and escorted through a private security line before entering the exclusive lounge, that quote resonated in my mind. These positive thoughts were a good sign, I thought.

Fast forward four days, I had an argument with a colleague that I respected highly, and I found myself doing something I had never done in my life before. I left our hotel in the morning, in a country I didn't know particularly well and a city I had never been to, found a bar and started drinking. I drank to take my mind off the stress that had been building up for months at that stage.

As I was in a largely different time zone, my wife wasn't yet awake and I was all alone.

There is no better way of saying this: Doing that scared the living shit out of me. I didn't know what came next. I didn't know if it was the start of a spiral I wouldn't have been able to turn around. All I really knew is it wasn't good.

The following morning I changed my flight and headed to the airport on my own. On the way home, in the accessible toilet at Belfast International Airport, I broke down. Uncontrollable tears, panic and anxiety combined with a fear I hadn't experienced before.

Why was that an important realisation? There are so many positive things we have in our businesses, but the negatives can be incredibly low. The pressure is real, and what I covered in this Chapter was a real game-changer for me to genuinely feel happy.

By having a qualified flow of prospects that were continually cleansed, where people were given the option to tell me they weren't interested and continued anyway, the quality of conversations I started having was amazing. I have fun with clients now, and that changed the way everything was framed in my head for the better.

Don't get me wrong, you still have to do the fucking work. There is no polite way of saying that. You have to deliver on what you do, but giving yourself a framework for your clients' experience can easily be the bedrock of that continued success.

What this meant was that on a recent trip to the airport, my entire mindset was completely different than that first trans-Atlantic trip to Austin. Because of the structure, I have for both my personal week and my prospects' journeys, and by thinking about things differently and from their perspective,

I have been able to see what others would see as negatives and turn them into positives.

A few years after my transatlantic trip, I travelled over to London for a football match, and the plan was to fly in the morning, head to the pub with my brother and father, attend the game, head for dinner with my parents and be on the 9:45pm flight home. Importantly, it was the day before my birthday, so I treated that trip a little birthday gift for myself.

All was going well until kick-off. The game was what can only be described as "typically disappointing." During the game, I received a notification that due to high winds and a storm affecting flights in and out of Belfast, my 9:45pm flight had been delayed to 11:55pm. But I still had to get to the airport on time, in case they found a new plane. I called the airline to see if I could simply move the flight to the following morning, but no luck.

I got to the airport and somehow was still in an incredible mood. I was so grateful for what I had as I headed into my 34th birthday that I was smiling to myself.

Sat in Luton airport, that delay went from 11:55pm to 12:20am, then jumped to 2:40am. At just before midnight, with the only people left in the airport the passengers on this sold-out flight, the notification on our phones that the flight was cancelled pinged in unison. We were stuck.

To make it worse, because of the storm, dozens of other flights had also been cancelled earlier in the day, meaning there was nothing from any London airport to Belfast for two days, and no flights from Luton airport for three.

I travel from Belfast to Birmingham on a regular basis, and I had a feeling no one else would check that route when thinking of what to do next, so I found one of a handful of seats on a flight out of Birmingham at 12:30pm the following day, which I jumped on. I had already accepted my fate, and while others around me were panicking or freaking out, I simply knew that it is what it is, so I might as well deal with it.

I was waiting at the desk to be let out of the airport and head to my parent's house for the night, with people around me getting irritated at admittedly a lack of communication from the staff, literally dancing to myself with music in one ear.

Even sat in Birmingham airport the following day, after another 3-hour+ delay, a last-minute gate change that literally was to the gate furthest away from where I was…but I was still happy. I spent a significant part of my birthday in an airport or travelling to and from one, completely unexpectedly.

I still finished the day feeling pure bliss, because despite the shit going on around me I was happy. Genuinely happy!

I want you to feel the happiness that comes from implementing things I have done.

"That's great, but how do you do it?" Here is the real meat of the strategy.

There are four steps to this, that when combined with everything learned in the book so far, can transform the entire process and how you approach business.

The steps are as follows:

1. Qualify your leads to the right places.
2. Purify your prospect list regularly.
3. Offer your prospects the opportunity to reject you where appropriate.
4. Structure your own time to accommodate the first three steps.

Qualification

So far you have learned that by viewing things from your prospects' perspective, where they don't care about you and the business, you can make things easy for them by setting expectations and utilising automation. This includes outlining clear next steps and planning their experience. By opening the floodgates this way, we end up attracting more interest, with less time being spent on repetitive manual tasks.

The fact still remains that not all leads (who are people, remember) are born equally. You are never going to convert 100% of those leads, and frankly nor should you. There comes a point where we need to direct and categorise leads in different ways.

Some businesses do this with intricate strategies of lead scoring, a practice whereby a prospect's actions cause them to have a set amount of points added to that score. Filled out a form? 15 points. Visited a website? 5 points. Opened an email? 2 points. Bought something before? 50 points. It can be a really effective way of having a solid, data-driven decision-making process that offers a sliding scale on customer value over their lifetime.

Whilst it can definitely be effective, it is quite an advanced way of handling it, and I want to offer a few more fundamental suggestions.

The way I have successfully done this is by breaking down what you have to offer into four main categories:

1. Free offerings that build a community,
2. low-ticket, low-effort offerings that can scale incredibly simply
3. mid-ticket, medium-effort offerings that can be scaled fairly easily, and
4. high-ticket, high-effort offering that is the "luxury yacht."

This doesn't mean to say you only have four products or services; far from it. But generally, most businesses can look at what they offer and put it into one of those four categories.

Free offerings that build a community are designed for those who are unlikely or unable to buy in the immediate future but are still a good fit for what you offer when the time comes. It could also be for people who are simply entering your world for the first time, potentially through those floodgates mentioned in the previous Chapter, with the aim of moving them from these free offerings to gradually more committed stages.

Low-ticket, low-effort offerings have to be incredibly reasonably priced but can't take up too much of your time, for example, membership fees or group mentorship programs whereby the entrance fee is nominal but the amount of time and effort you have to put in doesn't change, whether you have 1 attendee or 1,000.

Mid-ticket, medium-effort offerings are those that start to generate serious revenue for your business and do take effort to put together. But the sale of one is a big core for the business. For me, this is my consultation package, where I work with businesses to put teachings from this book into practice. It is an incredibly valuable offering to my clients while in actual time commitment for me it is only usually around 10 hours, meaning I can scale the number of clients I bring on without too much difficulty.

High-ticket, high-effort offerings, which I will often refer to as the "luxury yacht", are the more bespoke offerings, and will be a considered investment for anyone who decides to select it. They expect not only a return on that investment but a level of service that will blow them away. As such, your fees should reflect that.

Once you have what you offer separated into these categories, you now need to qualify your leads through your process into the one that suits them best.

For some, they may default to one of the categories based on the marketing campaign they originally responded to. For others, they may come to you directly for one of the higher offerings based on recommendations from previous clients or just your reputation as that grows. Either way, you can do this with automation by asking questions and using their answers to present relevant options.

For example, a client of yours could have a free book, an entry-level course at £99 or a high ticket £10,000+ offering. The specific offer they direct their prospects to can be heavily influenced by the answer to two questions: Are you looking to invest in what they offer in the future and how important is it to improve? Based on their answers and the choices they are given, they can be directed to any of their specific options. The goal is to deliver such high value to those in the lower categories that they are inclined to spend more and develop a closer working relationship.

By having your leads qualified into the right categories, you can focus your attention on the areas that make sense for you at the time. If generating cash fast is an important issue, you can reach out to the list of people who are in the top 2 categories and get some quick, high-value wins into the business.

When things are going well in that department, you can focus on additional time for tasks to scale out the lower ticket offerings and feed that system by opening more and more floodgates.

Purification

That initial step of categorising your leads is typically done actively at the start of a prospect's journey with your business or based on their most recent interaction with you.

Purification involves regularly monitoring and adjusting over time, and generally, this is done in one of two ways: periodic purges or countdown-based expiration.

Some businesses set aside time throughout the year to look back at their database and analyse what is in there, what still has potential and what should have been removed a long time ago. They will either remove people or re-categorise them.

This can be a great step to see where some missed opportunities lie, because getting someone to buy from you again and again is a surefire way of scaling the business beyond what you expected. After all, someone who has already spent money with you is likely to already trust you enough to do it again.

These "purges" are effective, although quite labour intensive, and a job that many people don't necessarily look forward to.

For others, especially those that use a lead scoring system, they have programmed a criteria into their scoring systems. After a certain time of inactivity, their lead's score drops until it eventually moves to 0. These can be equally as effective, and they take a lot less time once set up. Although they can sometimes be a little less personal and not take into account any interactions that the prospect has had with the business that isn't trackable.

Either way, having your database regularly cleansed leads to more effective marketing campaigns. The data you are using to base future decisions about scaling and the direction of the business also becomes much better informed.

Rejection

This is a step that most business owners seem to be scared of, but actually makes your life a lot simpler and easier.

Human beings are programmed generally to not be rude, and would rather lie to someone than face the awkward situation of telling them straight that they aren't interested. Think about a time that you have told a white lie to a friend to get out of plans that you didn't really fancy, or times that you have lied to a salesperson just to get off the phone rather than outright saying it isn't for you. We do this all the time, and the problem is, we don't feel we are being given a guilt-free option to say no.

Taking business out of the equation, imagine the following scenario: A friend of yours is looking to improve their own cooking as they are hoping to get into culinary school. So they invite you round to their house for an evening meal. Traditionally, they might invite you round and simply say, "I'm trying something new, so I'll cook, it would be great to have you guys round". Not a lot of clarity with the invitation, out of a sense of self-preservation and protection. After the meal, they ask, "What do you think?" to which you feel inclined to be nice and say only positive things. The problem occurs when the meal isn't good enough to make the cut for the school they were looking to get into.

A better way to approach the problem is for them to have said, "I'm looking at improving my cooking for a school I am applying to, so would love you to come over and try a new meal I have put together; I'll be expecting feedback too." In this scenario, they have set clear expectations in advance. After the meal, they ask, "What do you think? And please be honest because knowing what to improve will really help me." You will still include the positives, but you aren't held back and will give them the valuable constructive feedback they need to improve and get into the imaginary school I created for this example!

Bringing business back into it can be as simple as adding the two magical words to the end of a sentence: "Or not."

"Hi Chris, I'm calling today to see if we are still on for our sales call tomorrow or not?"

"I wanted to see if what I am doing over here would be a benefit to you and the business, or not."

"I have 10 tickets left, I need to see if you are interested, or not."

Giving someone the ability for a guilt-free rejection allows you to make sure those who are going into the different categories of Qualification are doing so of their own accord, and after having been given the chance to say no.

If at multiple points in their customer experience, they have been given the option to remove themselves from the interest they registered, and considering they don't care about you at the start of the process yet they are still moving further along, it is safe to say they are probably quite interested.

This step, done well and consistently, means that further down the line you are only speaking to people who are happy to be speaking to you, have clear expectations of why they are doing so in the first place, have a clear understanding of what the process looks like and have full clarity that it is their decision. This is because they were given enough opportunities to avoid the awkward situation when they weren't actually a good fit.

That change in the quality of conversation you are having with prospects, combined with the automation to save time on less productive interactions, has a massive impact on your business and your mental health.

You begin getting excited about those calls and enjoy the conversations, as they are with people who are looking forward to speaking to you, not dreading it because your expectations are misaligned.

Your time is being spent in a better mindset – one with clarity that you can help them and they are ready to hear how it works. In the next Chapter, I will detail how to structure these messages and the strategies for guiding people seamlessly through each step, which aligns with the content covered in all four steps mentioned above.

Structure

Once you have those three parts of the QPR theory in place, you need your own personal structure that can accommodate the influx of leads.

For some businesses reading this, you may have sales teams that will help delegate the tasks and split them across to ultimately improve that journey overall. For other businesses operated by one person, your time is your most valuable resource, which can quickly run out if you lack structure and open the floodgates.

I achieved this by putting a rigid structure into what I do. My weeks are laid out with certain days for certain things, something I learned initially from Nick James at an Expert Empires weekend business retreat, and further refined after reading Dan Sullivan's 10x is Easier Than 2x.

At the time of writing this book, my Mondays and Wednesdays are sales days. I take any call related to a potential sale or future relationship, as well as any sales practice, cold outreach or partnership discussions. By doing so, I can look at my calendar the day before and get excited by the fact that the day is full of sales calls. It also generally means the day will be profitable. I wake up in the morning knowing that all I am doing that day is sales, so I am in the right mindset throughout the day, which helps dramatically with how effective I am on those calls.

To see exactly how my weeks are laid out, send me the word **STRUCTURE** on WhatsApp.

The first day of sales being a Monday is no coincidence either; if I start my week with back-to-back sales calls, and I close from those calls, my week starts on the right foot, and everything else follows.

If you have ever had a great day at the start of a week, or a great meeting at the start of the day, and noticed that everything else went smoothly and easily for the rest of the week/day, it is because you were in the right mindset.

Before having that structure in place and taking calls on all days of the week, I could have a sales call with a perfect prospect ruined by a difficult meeting beforehand.

Tuesdays and Thursdays are client days, which are dedicated to consultation sessions and client work for larger projects. One worry I had when putting this element of the structure in place was that I felt I would be doing a disservice to my clients. As a people pleaser, it was always too easy for me to say "yes" to clients on days when I had space.

However, I realised that by being in the right headspace for client meetings, I was doing a better job on those meetings. I was a better teacher, a better problem solver and more effective at what I do. That was noticed by clients, and this meant I was able to clearly state that "the reason I take meetings on those two days is to maintain the quality of the service I offer while building the business and making sure I am still around to help.

On Fridays, I rarely take meetings, as they are my personal growth days, where I may listen to a new audiobook, go to the gym, or if the week has been a little more stressful it could be as simple as some time out with the family. On Saturdays and Sundays, I am usually off, with the exception of the last few hours of Sunday which I reserve for getting a head start on the week by clearing inboxes and getting on top of what happens that week.

This time is crucial to my week and has allowed me to focus on my own personal growth, which in turn affects what I do, what I offer and how effective I am at serving my clients.

Ask yourself this: What could you be doing with the extra time in your weeks if you structured everything correctly? How much would your business grow if you had time set aside each week to focus just on that? How much easier would dealing with your clients be if you had set boundaries they knew about, coming into working with you?

Perhaps a more probing question: Do you really want to be working 16 hours a day, seven days a week? Or would you rather have time set aside for your loved ones and the things that make you smile?

Now, I can be flexible with everything where needed, but the structure is set as the default, which helps me maintain the quality of what I am offering. It also allows me to effectively qualify, purify and encourage rejection from the leads that are coming into the business.

Combining everything means I have more time to myself, I have prospects who are happier and more qualified, who are ready to buy from me, as well as existing clients who are getting a high level of service despite more business being taken on, and my own mental health is as strong as it has ever been.

Chapter 14
What To Actually Say

Everything up to now in the book has been focusing on the reason and method behind what your customer's experience should look like. In this Chapter we will focus on what you need to say to be able to make that a success.

Having the right structure in place is the cornerstone of making this strategy a success, but it can all slip up if you don't know what to say and how to say it. That is a skill that you will need to develop, and which will come up as you understand more deeply how your prospects think.

Automation is a heavy theme throughout the book, and there are people who will say, "You can't automate that, people hate talking to robots." Those opinions are generally based on someone's experience with automation that was pretending to be a human, and that misalignment of expectations on yours and your prospect's side is ultimately where the experience falls down. How do you achieve that? By knowing what to say and how to say it.

It is vitally important that what you are saying is advancing the conversation with your prospect and enhancing their experience. The things that are said form the basis of their impression of your business, transitioning them from someone who doesn't give a shit about you to someone who is willing to invest money in you to help them solve a problem.

Remember, one thing or sentence taken the wrong way is an easy excuse for a prospect who doesn't care about you to give up and move on. It the same as when you had an experience with a business in the past that put you off using them, even though the positives outranked the negatives.

I am going to detail what questions you should be asking, how you should ask them, the importance of when you ask them and why they should be asked in the first place.

If you have gone to write an email and not been sure what to say, or record a video/voice note to a prospect to advance the conversation, this Chapter will help with a few golden nuggets of things to ask and how to ask them.

A lot of the inspiration behind this Chapter has been from my ongoing education with a fantastic sales trainer Matt Elwell, and the ethical way he teaches people to sell. His book, *Open With A Close* dives into a lot more depth on sales strategy when you are speaking to people in general, and elements of this Chapter focus on how to frame that conversation by saying the right things in the build up to those calls.

I want to start with the following sentence:

"I didn't tell you to kill him."

This sentence is simple enough, albeit slightly ominous. It is seven words that aren't complicated. However, there are SIX different meanings behind this sentence, simply based on how you say it.

I want you to read the following versions of the sentence by putting emphasis on the word that is underlined. In doing so, you will see completely contrasting meanings behind the same seven-word sentence:

<u>I</u> didn't tell you to kill him.
You are saying that you were not the person who instructed the killing, implying that someone else was likely the person who instructed you to bring this poor person to their demise.

I didn't tell you to kill him.

Clearly, a misunderstanding has happened, and you are adamant that the exact opposite of what has likely happened was your intention.

I didn't tell you to kill him.

I may well have suggested to off the poor lad, but I didn't explicitly tell you that is what you should do.

I didn't tell you to kill him.

Clearly, I was under the impression that someone else should have the honour of ending this man. How could you steal that from them?!

I didn't tell you to kill him.

Perhaps I suggested you scare or threaten him, not end his life. Dobby didn't mean to kill anyone. Dobby only meant to maim or seriously injure.

I didn't tell you to kill him.

A classic case of mistaken identity, you have brought a seemingly innocent person to meet their maker when clearly you should have been offing someone else.

Either way, this poor lad is not having a great week.

The issue is that you could have written that sentence with one intention, and realistically that is only one of six possible options, and you are leaving the recipient of the message to interpret the sentence to come to a conclusion.

A literal dice role of options, and an over 83% chance that they will get it wrong.

Have you ever read an email from a co-worker and thought something wildly negative, only to find out you misread the email entirely and it was completely innocent? Ever received a message from a friend that meant something completely different to what you thought? Ever read a status on someone's social media and put an interpretation on the meaning behind it, and find out later you were completely off the mark? Of course, it happens all the time.

It is incredibly difficult to read someone's tonality in a written message unless they make it blindingly obvious, and for that to happen they have to realise in the first place that the message could be taken in multiple ways, something that often isn't clear.

Combine that with the fact your prospects don't give a shit about you, and you have someone who is inclined from the initial point of contact to not want to read your message in a positive light.

We are more likely to misread an email from a colleague we don't like than one we do. We are more likely to misread a message from someone when we aren't in a good mood versus when we are on cloud nine.

Your prospect's reading of your message can be influenced by countless factors that are neither in your control nor known by you at all. Remember, you will never know the reason people don't buy unless they explicitly tell you, and even then that is if they are being bluntly honest and not trying to be nice.

There are passages in this book that will have been written in a tonality that lives in my head, that you will have read completely differently. The Dobby reference above either went right over your head, or you read it in the accent of a fictional house elf. I will never know which one, and I will never know which of you read that sentence and smiled a little. Does this count as breaking the fourth wall?

How do get past this issue then? I feel it is a combination of a few things: the types of questions you ask, the choices you give your prospects, the medium with which you deliver the message and the personality you have to deliver these messages.

I will state now that there are copywriters out there who will read elements of this Chapter and throw the book at a wall, and for that, I simply say it is easier to ask forgiveness than permission.

For ease, I have broken this strategy into four steps.

Step 1: Don't Let Them Say No

Many salespeople suggest this but for the wrong reasons. They aim to turn a no into a yes or ask really leading closed questions that a normal person couldn't reasonably say no to. "Do you want your life to be better by earning more money?", "Would you benefit from higher revenue every month?", "If we got you x3 more revenue every month, you wouldn't complain would you?"

I hate these questions. They are designed to get people to say yes, and the implication is the more times someone says yes, the more positive they will be when they ask the "Are you ready to buy and change your life?" question. It makes me feel a little sick in the back of my mouth.

What I mean by not letting them say no is asking powerful questions that allow the prospect to create their own vision of what success could look like. Questions that generate information and feedback that will ultimately help you to see if you can help them, and help the prospect build trust in you.

Instead of asking the question "Are you looking to generate more sales by working together?" which seems like you are trapping someone into an answer, you could ask "What are you looking to achieve if we do some business together?" As long as what they are looking for is something you can actually deliver on, then great, we have the chance to do business.

Instead of asking the question, "Would you like more information?" you could say, "The next step is for me to send over some information on packages, where is the best place to send it?"

Instead of asking, "Will you be the one making the decisions?" ask instead, "Who needs to be in the decision-making process if we were to do some business together?"

These questions remove the word no from your prospect's possible replies, and someone who doesn't care about you – as has been the theme for the entire book – is likely to want to lean towards the negative. Remember, as we learned in the last Chapter, giving them the option to remove themselves from the process by telling you they aren't interested is a powerful tool here.

The key is to make sure your prospects are in a state of choice during the conversation, something often at odds with what most gurus teach. This brings us to step 2.

An important point to mention is that these questions should be outcome-based. They should always be designed to progress the conversation forward and further down the sales process. One of the best examples I have heard Matt Elwell state is the question, "What is your biggest challenge in business right now?" It is incredibly vague and hard to answer because it could refer to any number of things that have nothing to do with the thing you offer. If you offered automation, you could say, "When it comes to saving time within your business, what is your biggest challenge in business right now?"

Your job is to serve your prospects by helping them identify problems they might have through the questions you ask, so make sure they are outcome-based.

Step 2: Give Them Choices

When you are speaking to a prospect directly, the questions you will ask can be a lot more open than when they are delivered through automation.

The questions above are powerful questions, but also easy ones to leave open. A prospect can just ignore them or forget about them later in the day. They can also go off on a number of different tangents, something that standard non-AI-driven automation can often fall victim to, and at that stage, you are likely going to lose their interest.

This is where we bring choices into the mix, something that keeps the prospect on the right track.

Imagine for a moment you are planning the route someone would need to take from one city to another. If there was just endless flat land between point A and point B, you could just say "Drive straight, you'll get there eventually." But along that route, your prospect can feel like they don't know where to go next, or they don't trust your advice even though you know best.

If you put them on a road with clear markings, widely understood standards of driving and obvious repeated signage, then they will be able to do that journey with ease.

You have to do that in your customer's journey, by offering them choices they are willing to pick.

Instead of asking the question, "Do you want to have a meeting?" you could say, "The next step is for us to have a meeting. I have time on Monday or Wednesday, which is best for you?" Someone who wants to have a meeting simply needs to choose between the days, not between yes or no, where 50% of the options don't help you. Of course, they won't say no, they will say "Oh, I'm not sure, let me check my calendar and get back to you."

Instead of saying, "You just need to pay now, is that ok?" you could say, "The next step is payment. Which would you prefer, card or bank transfer?"

"Are you ready to sign?" becomes "Based on the information you have, which package would suit you best and bring the best results?".

I often have a demo of what I offer in the form of a WhatsApp chatbot that asks users to pick a card through a series of messages. The first question teases them by showing off what it can do and showing a clear expectation (Chapter 10) that they will answer a few questions. At the end of it, I will send them a picture of their card. No one who has started that process has ever failed to complete it.

It asks a series of questions, explaining as it goes what the purpose is. At the end, it asks a question with three options: 1) I could use this, 2) It won't work for me, and 3) I have questions.

If the first option is pressed it says, "Great to hear, the next step is to book a meeting" and sends a link where they have the choice of a time that suits them.

The 2nd option is my way of qualifying them out, while option 3 says, "Questions are great, how would you like to ask them?" and presents two further options to remain chatting, or whether they want to book a call.

By the end of the little demo, I have set expectations and explained everything I do, showed what it can look like, made it really easy for them to book a call, got them to engage with me through a chat (which is my next logical step), qualified whether they would be a good fit or now, improved the quality of their time spent looking at and engaging with my business and increased the time they have spent looking at my business, which makes a big difference initially. They are slowly going from "I don't give a shit" to "Ooh, this looks interesting." That is a seismic shift in mindset and mentality for a prospect at the start of their journey with your business. Get them to shift that mentality, and you already have a much higher chance of closing them as a sale.

To experience my process demo, send me the word **DEMO** on WhatsApp.

Be aware, however, that too many choices will give your prospects decision paralysis, a mistake that is often made by businesses that want to cover all the bases possible. If you have ever scrolled through your Netflix and struggled to pick a movie or TV show, you will know what that feels like. We find it much easier to pick a film at a cinema if you decide to go out for the evening simply because there is a limited amount of choice.

With that in mind, be specific about your choices that are on offer, and don't back your prospects into a corner that they don't feel comfortable with.

Step 3: The Medium is Important

This bit might make a few people a little uncomfortable, but it is what will separate you from your competition: You need to make your voice heard.

I started this Chapter by explaining how one seven-word sentence can be misunderstood in six different ways. But it is understood completely and instantly when it is said out loud with the appropriate inflection.

The words you say are important, but the manner in which you say them is equally important. I previously talked about being confident as part of your process, and in reality that confidence can be heard in someone's voice a lot easier than when it is read in a text-based message.

Hearing someone sounding confident is much more likely than reading a message that is written confidently. In written messages, there is a fine line between confidence and arrogance, and that line is much more easily navigated when you can hear the tonality of the other person.

I choose to do a lot of this message delivery via video in WhatsApp, a lot of which I can automate, for a number of reasons. First, there is an authenticity about seeing someone that you simply can't get in any other manner. Speaking to someone in person in real life is the easiest way to build a connection, yet that isn't always possible. For me, the next best thing is video.

We humans read a lot into what we observe, often with a lot of our observations being subconscious. If you've ever felt a little "off" when speaking to someone, or you can't quite put your finger on why you don't trust the person you are talking to, it is because your intuition is a powerful tool, and it is informed by every sense you have access to.

From a video we can hear tonality, understand the meaning behind the words that are being said, see a friendly face, fill in the gap in our head we may have on what someone looks like, and read body language. We can virtually look them in the eyes and feel either at ease with the conversation or be put off if it isn't done well.

It may not be nice, but we judge people on their appearance. Not specifically as an attraction to someone, but seeing if they take care of themselves if they are wearing professional clothing. We may not want to admit it, but it comes into play.

It would be frankly incorrect to not state that people buy from people they are attracted to a lot easier. And whilst I am definitely not putting a section in the book saying, "Be attractive, so that people will buy from you" – mainly because people buy from me and I look like a recently unearthed potato on some days – we make our decisions on if we trust people based on a lot less.

A video at the start of their interaction with your business can build a conscious and subconscious connection that an email alone, saying "Thanks for your enquiry, we will be in touch," would struggle to achieve.

A video sent 24 hours before a sales call that outlines what is going to happen on the call in a clear, concise way sets expectations and makes sure the prospect is aligned. It is an incredibly powerful tool as part of the customer journey.

Now, if you are reading this and the thought of recording a video for people to see as part of their sales process is giving you the cold sweats, there are ways around it.

One simple way is to get someone else in your team to record the video, someone who is more confident on camera and can deliver the questions and the message in a much better way.

This is important; if you aren't confident and trustworthy in that video, it can have the opposite impact. So if you are truly not good in front of a camera, trying to force the issue can negatively affect the customer experience.

If you don't have anyone in your team, you can outsource it to an actor or a media company to do it for you. The cost of doing so will typically be a one-off cost, and the confidence they will have on camera will definitely help, provided you have done Steps 1 & 2 well enough to give them the right things to say.

Failing video and voice notes on messaging platforms have a great impact too. These are particularly useful in follow-up after they have seen you and built their opinion of your body language and appearance. It is easy to convey your message and ask powerful questions when you use your voice, and the prospect can hear you and understand the meaning behind what you are asking a lot more clearly.

Step 4: Have A Personality, Don't Be Boring!

I love the following quote: "There is no point trying to be someone else; everyone else is already taken, you might as well be you."

This could be a whole other book about being comfortable in being you, but for now, you simply need to understand this: Your ideal customer, whom you enjoy working with, is much more likely to actually work with you if they like the person they are speaking to. They can only like the real you if that is what is presented to them.

I've often found it ironic that society teaches us to try and be people we are not, to attract people who see the person we are trying to be, not the person we are. While doing so we put off those people who are looking for the person we actually are, because they don't think we are that person.

Either way, in the context of your prospect's experience, you have to inject a little bit of your personality there. Answer this question: Do you have competition? Thought so. And to be successful, you have to stand out among your competition. The easiest way to do that is to be you.

As your business grows, the "personality" of the business often gets diluted as a result of a number of factors. C-suite executives who don't believe in anything other than the suit-and-tie, formal everything approach. Committees of people working on the business's "tonality." A dozen people add different things into the mix so that the business sounds disjointed and mismatched. It isn't easy, but the important things rarely are.

You have to have an identity, a personality that connects with your prospect and what they are looking for. As a solo entrepreneur, this is easy. You are you. Be you.

Your job with that personality is to let it shine! Don't have your boring messages that every one of your competitors has by default – stand out! You have a core belief that people should be buying from you rather than your competitors, and giving them a reason to do so other than "we are the cheapest" is part of a core successful business that can scale.

This can be from little touches – such as different text on buttons that typically would say something generic like "book now" – all the way up to gifts that you send when someone comes on board and purchases your offering.

Be bold! You have a prospect who currently does not care about your business, and your job is to turn them into an advocate for your business who will, without hesitation, recommend you to everyone they know. The easiest way to do that is to offer great service and be different in how you deliver it.

Only you know your personality, therefore only you will be able to work out how that should come across. But a general rule of thumb is that if you are writing emails or messages differently from how you would say the exact same thing if someone were in front of you, you are likely a bit misaligned yourself.

A lot of this book has focused on understanding the mentality your prospect has at the start of their journey with you, and the importance of a system that is consistent for them to follow. But all of that systemisation falls down if you are saying the wrong thing through the process. And even if you are saying the right thing, it could be taken the wrong way if it isn't being delivered in a manner that they want to receive it.

In relationships, you can refer to it as the "uh oh" moment. Any doomed relationship has a moment where something happens, whether it is something that has been said or an action that has been done that ultimately puts you off

When I was 14, I remember going on a date with a girl I had been introduced to. I was excited and travelled from northwest London to south London to meet up. We had been speaking over messages, and getting to know each other. As a 14-year-old, a lot of this was new and it was daunting, to say the least.

I turned up, we got on a bus to head to our destination for the day, and after a few stops an old lady stepped into the bus and asked the driver if the bus went to a specific area of town. It was clear the driver wasn't sure if it did or not, as it wasn't a specific stop or road that was being asked about. I, not knowing the area at all, didn't have a clue. The old lady stepped off the bus and waited at the bus stop in hopes of a bus coming along that might take her to where she needed it. This was well before the days of phones with good enough internet connection that could bring up a map and I could help.

As the bus pulled away, my date leaned over to me and told me that she knew that location, and the bus did in fact go there, but she said, "The lady looked like she smelled, so I didn't say anything." I was mortified inside, and it completely changed my entire emotion. I look back and wish I had the confidence as a 14-year-old boy just to stand up, get off the bus and leave, but alas I didn't and continued with the date. All throughout I knew this was the last time we were going to meet up, and a few hours later I made my excuses and left.

That moment was one fleeting sentence that gave me a whole different perspective, and whilst that is a clear example of our values being misaligned, it could have easily been a joke on her side that I simply misinterpreted. Fourteen feels like a long time ago now.

My emotion changed despite being excited about the date, and emotion is rarely the first port of call for your leads.

That "uh oh" moment for your business could be one sentence that doesn't ring true with what your prospect is looking for. It could be one missing bit of information that could easily be put in the message you are sending to your prospects as they are enquiring.

Run a pub that is dog-friendly? If that isn't advertised and I am looking for a pub to stop at on walks with the dog, I won't step inside.

Need a restaurant that has a gluten-free option? If you call the restaurant and the person on the other phone says, "Yes, we have gluten-free options" then great! If they say, "We probably have gluten-free options", the chances are you are looking for an alternative. Nothing like a bit of doubt to put someone off buying from you.

Give money to those you trust

I ask this question again: When was the last time you gave money to a business when you doubted if they could deliver what you needed? Your messaging needs to do a lot of heavy lifting when it comes to your customer's experience. It needs to be engaging, clear, unambiguous, conversation-invoking and natural, all at the same time. What you say matters, and how you say it matters.

Imagine being at the altar, and when asked the question, "Do you take this person to be your lovingly wedded spouse?" You answered, "I do?" with an inflection on the word do that sounded like you were asking a question. Sounding unsure with those two words could genuinely be the seed of doubt that causes a whole relationship to crumble to the ground.

Equally, with the same example, timing is incredibly important. You could say the words "I do" in the exact right tonality, but if it takes you a minute to get them out...Houston, we have a problem!

It is important to follow up on your leads more than you think, but doing eight follow-ups in one day is going to get you blocked, regardless of how well-written and vocally delivered your messaging is.

When you are planning and designing your follow-up sequences, which we will bring together in the last Chapter, you need to make sure the space between the outreach effectively is reflected in the messaging. A follow-up that goes out a month after the first meeting will have different tonality, content and urgency than one that goes out 24 hours after the proposal has been sent to them for example.

Equally, if a message is in the build-up to a set timed event, a bit of urgency in that message is expected and should be reflected in everything you put together.

The main takeaway from this Chapter should be that you use your messaging, language and delivery of the content to develop a better understanding of your prospect. A previous Chapter covered the importance of understanding your prospects, and there is no better way to do that than asking powerful questions that elicit a response and drive the conversation – whether that ends with them qualifying themselves out of your process or a seamless sale that is easy and simple for everyone involved.

Chapter 15
You've Got the Ingredients, Let's Bake That Cake!

This book started with the idea that once you realise your prospects truly don't give a shit about your business, you will be able to build a customer experience that converts more leads into sales and saves you time. Every Chapter so far has formed the building blocks to achieve just that, and this Chapter is designed to bring that all together.

You have the ingredients in what you have read already, but the cake is what we really want. Let's bake a cake!

We've all had poor experiences with businesses, more often than not because of communication being poor. It is one of my biggest irritations when a business knows something and doesn't share it with the person interacting, which could ultimately improve their experience.

The rarer you make that reaction to your business, the more likely people are to buy from you.

Initially, you realise that no one really cares about you and what you do, only the problem you could potentially solve. They are defaulted to be negative, so anything that induces a negative reaction will kill the chances of them buying from you early

Next, I showed you that those leads we always talk about are actual humans, with lives that get in the way, and priorities a lot higher than spending money with you. Once you remember that, you will adjust your own perspective from "they aren't interested" to "maybe they just have a busy life." Following that, you started looking into what is natural for them to do anyway and making sure that whatever you put into practice is designed to make it easy for them to act, knowing that they don't care and what kind of person they naturally were.

Once you understand that they don't always want everything as fast as possible, they just want to have their expectations set and met by the company they are investing money in, the quality of their experience is more important than the speed. That is where automation plays a vital role because it is impossible to set everyone's expectations manually, especially as you start to scale.

Once that understanding is there, the technicalities of what your automation should look like combined with being more persistent than you think – because they don't care and they have their own lives – become an important aspect of what happens.

The planning of those steps becomes essential once you have the understanding of why they need to be put in place, and setting clear logical steps throughout by delivering confident and consistent messaging is how you achieve it.

Once that is planned out, you can start scaling the elements of the business that bring in the leads. Use the correct messaging, questions, and choices to guide your leads to the destination you ultimately want them to reach.

Micro-Experiences Drive Business Impact

Every touch point that a prospect has with your business – from a visit to a webpage to a form completion, an email reading to a social media post – will impact their impression of you and what they are likely to do moving forward. I call these small touch points "micro-experiences." They are usually things most businesses don't have the time or resources to properly design and create, while together they form the entire impression that a prospect has.

The better each of these micro-experiences is, the better the chances of them wanting to buy from you, and the more they will begin to trust you.

How many times have you returned to a business and bought from them again based on something that was seemingly small in the grand scheme of things? A helpful member of staff, someone remembering your name, a funny sign, a little gift. Something unique that stood out, that on its own doesn't form the basis of whether you buy from them again, but is the thing you recount to anyone you are recommending the business to.

"The food was great, and one of the waiters remembered my birthday, we have to go back."

"The lady that cares for our dogs is amazing, and she always leaves a little bow on their collar when we get them back."

"The zoo was great, and there was a funny sign that said, 'Don't enter the enclosure, the monkeys will eat you and that will make them sick.'"

These are all things I have said about businesses I have interacted with, and you will have examples of micro-experiences that you have had with your favourite businesses. These are priceless and very hard to quantify, and can only be implemented when you have given yourself enough time to focus on them by understanding and automating your customer journey.

Here are my 5 keystones to implementing the learnings in this book, and what needs to be done to succeed.

Keystone 1: "What Do I Want Them To Do?" vs. "What Are They Likely To Do?"

Too many businesses focus on what they want a prospect to do. It's a logical question, and one that shouldn't be ignored, but it should definitely not be the only question you are asking.

If the aim is to get a prospect to book in a call with your team, you should think at each stage what they are likely to do. If they enquire, they are likely to want to know more, so deliver what they want to know. If that question is answered, what are they likely to do? They are likely to want their problem to be solved, so your job is to tell them what can be done (providing you genuinely can solve it for them, and if not you qualify them out of your pipeline), and what the next steps look like. Then it is about making it easy for them to do so.

When are they likely to want a meeting? How are they likely to book it? What can you put in place that makes that the easiest and most obvious decision for them?

If all you think about is that you want to get them to book a call, you will miss how to actually get them to do it.

By asking the question "What are they likely to do?" at each step of your customer journey, you will start to fill in the cracks that your prospects were previously dropping off at. Each drop-off point you identify and help secure means more prospects get further along the process. The further everyone gets, the more likely they all are to buy from you.

Thinking about each of those micro-experiences they are going to have with your business, you need to ask the question "What are they likely to do?" What path are they likely to take? What emotion are they likely to have? What problem do they have at that moment, not overall?

If you approach each of these steps with the understanding you have learned in the first few Chapters, you are on the right track.

Keystone 2: Align With Everything Where Possible

When you are on the same wavelength as your prospects, good things happen for everyone. From your core values to their expectations, any misalignment will ultimately either cause a sale to fall through or a problem post-sale.

My core values are clear to me and are written down wherever possible. No one who works with me can do so without both knowing my values, but also agreeing that they align with them.

You know that feeling you get when you are speaking to someone, and something feels a little off? You can't place what that is, but you have a feeling that if you work together, it won't go well. That is almost always because your values aren't aligned. And that is completely ok, you aren't designed to work with everyone. Trying to force yourself to work outside of that value is not a positive to your life.

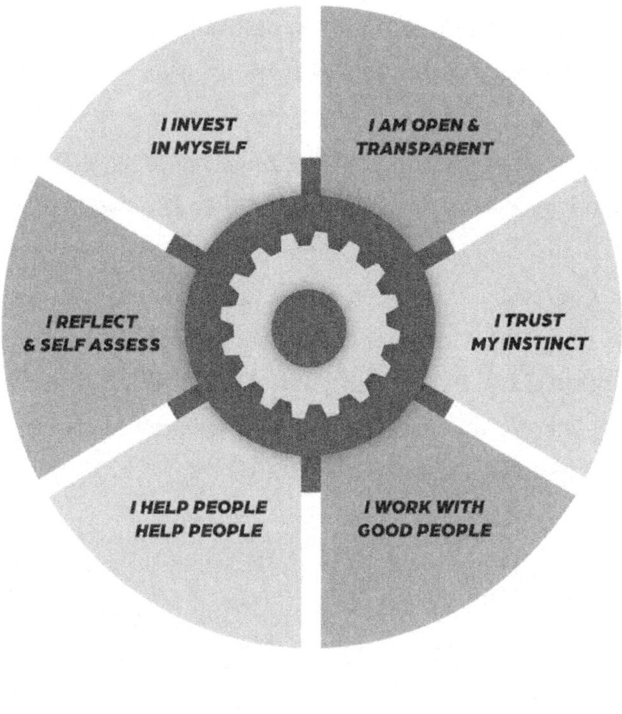

My core values are as follows:

- I reflect and self assess, so I can continue to grow
- I invest in myself, both time and money in training and development
- I work with good people, those that fill me with joy
- I help people help people, so my impact has a ripple effect
- I trust my instinct because it is so rarely wrong
- I am open and transparent because I believe in relationships and trust

These values are non-negotiable and are what I hold myself to. If I don't feel right in a situation, I remember my values and work out which one isn't aligning.

When you are putting your customer journeys in place, they should be designed to find those that align with you and eliminate those that don't align with them. You may want to put your values down on paper the same way I do, or you may know them in your heart. But designing each part of your prospect's experience with your values in mind is important – not only for the quality of their experience but also for your own mental health moving forward.

Aligning with values is not the only important thing. Expectations being both set and either met or exceeded is the cornerstone of relationship building.

I once worked with a ticket seller in Mallorca, and his strategy behind selling tickets was to lie. He set such unrealistic expectations of the event he was selling that it caused problems further down the line for all of us to deal with.

The event itself was incredibly entertaining, and most people who attended it loved it. He didn't need to lie and missell the event, but it became part of his nature. I argued with him a lot because some of the things he said were ridiculous. We would often get hen parties and large groups of ladies at the event, and to get them to buy would mean a good level of commission for him. We could comfortably give them a slight discount and throw in a bottle of prosecco, but I remember one boat where he had promised all 10 ladies in the group a bottle of champagne each. And not the standard house prosecco we had, a bottle of "anything they wanted", quoting directly from the angry maid of honour we had to deal with about 15 minutes into the event. The expectations being misaligned caused us problems that impacted sales for future events.

Those expectations need to be clear at every step of your process, from telling them what they will receive when filling out a form and enquiring to what the financial options are when they are ready to buy. There is kindness in the clarity of telling people what is going to happen.

"Fill this form in and I will send you the information immediately. After that we will give you the option to see what it could be like to work together, should that be of interest." This approach is so much more enjoyable for your leads to go through, is so much better at qualifying those who aren't interested, and leads to better conversations further down the line. The moment you break the expectation with your prospect, they will immediately abandon the process. Simple as that.

With that in mind, lay out expectations that you can only ever meet or exceed. If you usually get back to someone within 24 hours, but sometimes it takes 48 hours, don't tell your prospects it is usually 24 hours. Tell them it will be within 48 hours, because the second you enter hour 25, they will lose trust. And someone who doesn't give a shit about you losing trust early on isn't something that often benefits you.

Align your expectations and your values with theirs, and the world will be a better place for you to be in.

Keystone 3: Automate Where Possible, Delegate Where Necessary

You simply can't scale a business without automation, and your prospect's experience with you will only ever be enhanced when the automation they go through as micro-experiences is built with them in mind.

The biggest impact I feel automation can have on you and the business is your time. Time is the one resource that no one has more of than anyone else. We all have the same amount of hours a day, days in a week, weeks in a year. What you can achieve in that time is down to how well you manage that time.

Jobs that are repetitive, may only take a few minutes here and there but happen all the time, and need to either be automated or delegated. Your job is to grow the business, and you aren't able to do that if you don't have the time to do it.

Have you ever been on holiday, then come back feeling refreshed and like you can conquer the world in business? That is because you have taken the time out from the business to recharge and refresh. Ask yourself this question: If taking time out from working in the weeds has a good impact on your business, why on earth would you not do it more often?

Most people answer it the same way, in that tasks need to be done and the business still needs to run day in, day out.

I call this the Irony of Time Cycle. It's the notion that you don't have the time to implement strategies that would ultimately free up more time to grow your business.

Automation will allow time to be freed up, which I implore you to use to grow the business, not just work more hours within it. Because if all you are doing in the business is working the jobs and not growing, then you don't have a business – you have a job.

Keystone 4: Take Some F*cking Action

There is no understating this point; if you don't put into action the things you *know* will benefit the business at the time you are most inspired by them, you won't do it.

I attend a lot of conferences, and at those events, there are always a few bits of brilliant information that I take away. Many people who attend the same events know what that looks like, but if I don't set aside time to actually implement those things, they will never happen.

In 2021, I was at a business conference and heard an expert talking about TikTok. I can't remember most of the talk, but the one thing I do remember is a statistic that he gave. At that time, according to him, 52% of TikTok users in the UK were over the age of 25. That blew my mind, because up to that point, I assumed TikTok was full of 14-year-olds dancing, and frankly people that shouldn't be watching 14-year-olds dancing. That one statistic caused me to create a TikTok account. But having an account wasn't taking action.

In the foyer of the hotel, during the break, I recorded my first ever TikTok. It got over 80,000 views, and was the story of my business at the time. Now, I post 2-3 videos per day on the platform, and enquiries from purely organic views have made me £10,000s. All because I took action when I was most inspired.

If you are planning on attending events in the future to get ideas to grow the business, block out a day from the business following the event with the pure intention of implementing or beginning the implementation of ideas you haven't even had yet. Act on your inspiration at the time you are most inspired.

If any part of this book has made you rethink how you approach things and you want to put it into action, get your diary out now and put the time in your calendar to implement the learnings. I'll be here when you get back.

Running a business is hard. People don't talk about it anywhere near enough, you only see the positive side of it on social media. But juggling everything that comes with your business, plus the pressure of the mouths you have to feed, isn't an easy route to take. If it was, there would be more business owners in the general population, and you wouldn't be in the minority.

Growing a business is even harder, but to do so you have to put the time in to focus on growth, not just working in the business. Sure, there are some occasions when businesses boom for reasons they had no control over. If you made hand sanitiser, 2020 was a great year for you! You weren't the reason for the success, but you were in the right place at the right time. Most businesses don't have the once-in-a-generation event of a global pandemic to boost sales; in fact, many businesses folded under the same circumstances.

But growing your business is damn near impossible if you aren't doing these three things: thinking about your customers first, setting aside time to actually focus on that growth, and learning from others around you.

Your customers are first because they give you money. We can talk about the bigger picture of building a community all we want, but at the end of the day, getting your prospects to spend money with your business is the only way you generate revenue.

Setting aside time to focus on a strategy for growth is not only common sense, it would be ridiculous if you didn't agree with it. I mentioned Usain Bolt earlier, and I can guarantee he didn't just wake up one day and run that speed. He set aside time to focus on growing his abilities. Jeff Bezos isn't working on the factory line packing up orders for customers in Amazon, he is only dedicating his time to meetings that are designed to further the growth of Amazon. If you aren't setting that time aside, ask yourself this: What do you need to do to get the time to focus on growing the business? Write down three answers, and just fucking do them.

And learning from others is so incredibly important I don't know why it isn't done more often. Taking aside the fact learning from the right people is a factor here, which it definitely is, but absorbing information from those who have actually succeeded in what they do is almost guaranteed to give you insights that you didn't have before. You have made it this far into the book, and you are still here because something caused you to keep reading. If there aren't one or two nuggets of information that you have garnered from reading the book, the chances of you getting this far aren't high, so my advice with those nuggets is to action them today.

Keystone 5: Reevaluate Regularly

Things change quickly in the world, quicker than they ever have before. I have the privilege of saying I am older than Google, and there is an entire generation that couldn't imagine a world without it.

I like pointing out to businesses the following: If your target market is people aged 25 to 30, then every five years your entire target audience is completely different people.

Previously, we covered that people generally do one of three things: what they have always done, what feels natural for them to do, and what they think everyone else is doing. What feels natural can change over time; using QR codes was something that, pre-pandemic, wasn't as popular. But the combination of having to scan one to enter a restaurant and the fact that major mobile phone providers started building it into their camera features, eliminating the need for a new app, massively changed our behaviour.

Blockbuster is a great example of this. If you are unfamiliar with the story of Blockbuster then firstly, thank you for making me feel old. In the late '90s, going to Blockbuster on a Friday night to pick a movie was an elite-level weekend entertainment plan. They were packed, and you had to time going there correctly to make sure there wasn't too much of a queue.

The owners of Blockbuster were focused on scaling, and they rapidly went to place as many stores around the globe as they could. In the USA, they peaked in 2005 with just over 5,700 stores nationwide.

But the biggest mistake they made was in two parts. Firstly, they didn't reevaluate what they were doing in enough depth, and secondly, they didn't take into account what people were likely to do. There was a trend emerging as the internet started becoming faster and more accessible.

They had the opportunity to be the Netflix of the world. Not just because they had a strong brand with the recognition that could blow anyone out of the water, and not just because they had the connections in the industry to make the streaming of films a little bit easier, but because they were actually pitched the idea by the now co-founders of Netflix!

Fast forward 10 years they had less than 40 stores, and by 15 years they had just one novelty store remaining. A blockbuster fall from grace, if ever there has been one.

Anything that you put into practice from this book, or any other books for that matter, you should reevaluate regularly. Factor in the time in your diary for regular looks back to see what is and what isn't working. Learn from what you have seen and what the data says. That data is important too – you've read throughout this book about getting people from one step to the next in the easiest way possible, but having discernable data to track where those prospects are disappearing will be what tells you the areas you need to improve and the impact any changes are having.

I do this by blocking out a day every month, two days every quarter and three days every year to simply look at everything in the business and see where I can improve. These days are non-negotiables, and to make it so that I stick to them, I block out a hotel meeting room just to work on them. Financially committing to the days really helps me keep on track; "I've spent money on this room, I'm getting my money's worth!"

On top of that, every week I set myself a 1% task, something small that I can add that may improve the business by 1%, knowing that enough of those 1% increases over time will mean my business will double.

One of my core values is *I reflect and self-assess* because I truly believe that without being open to receiving, evaluating, and learning from criticism, I can't grow both personally and professionally.

I guarantee you, any changes you put into your business as a result of this book, you will revisit in the next six months, whether that is because your prospects are starting to show you trends you didn't realise before, or you start developing it in more depth, aiming to go from 0 to 80, then 80 to 85 and increasing from there.

What It All Means for You

Over the last few years, I have done everything I can to absorb information and put it into practice in both my business and professional life. The learnings have meant I am the happiest person I have ever been, and I am financially doing better than I could have imagined. I put that success down to the principles laid out in this book: Understand your prospects, improve their experience, and ask them the right questions. Do this, and they will actually start giving a shit about you!

I have more time with my family, to deliver smiles to the faces of those I love. I have better professional and personal relationships with those around me, which brings me joy and pride. I have a level of patience and calmness that is ever present in my day-to-day life with the exception of being at the football on the weekends.

Once I started understanding my prospects and their behaviour, things clicked in a way that I couldn't believe. I also couldn't understand why no one was doing the same thing, and if I am honest I still don't know why this isn't being spoken about as much. What I do know is if every business approached their customers by understanding who they are, what they need, what they are likely to do and the fact they don't give a shit about the business, every customer's experience would be better. And if we as customers enjoy it, then everyone will be happier.

Conclusion

In the first few Chapters of the book, you will have reframed how you think about prospects and people interacting with your business, and have an understanding that they are real human beings who value their time and need things made very easy for them.

You will also have an understanding that automation in your customer journey is essential, why that is the case and how you should (and shouldn't) implement it.

We have explored the importance of planning out that journey and working out the smaller logical next steps of your experience, as well as what you are putting in those automations to give you the highest chance of creating a conversation and connection between you and your prospects.

Finally, we have brought all of that together to create one fluid customer journey, with the aim of making your prospects' and customers' interactions with your business be as smooth, easy and enjoyable as possible. This in turn will lead to more sales, less stress and more time for you to work on the business.

The point of such a granular look at their experience is when you start implementing things into your business, and do so with the customer experience at its heart, you will see success. You will see more people talking about how good the process is, how much they felt looked after, and how pleasurable it was to give you money.

That's a somewhat alien concept to most, but you will know you have done this right when people start saying, "I spent more than I was expecting but I am happy I did." Not a bad sentence to hear back at all.

When there is a consistent journey that all of your prospects will experience, that is smooth, easy and enjoyable, you can start funnelling people into that process at a rate that before felt unobtainable.

Plus, having people who are happy interacting with you as a business has a wider impact. You will raise the bar for which your customer interactions should be, which makes everyone a little happier.

When done well, this happiness with interactions will increase the morale of your team, as they are dealing with people who are excited to be on calls with you.

As you look to implement any changes to your business, ask yourself this question: How will my customer's experience change if we implement this?

The quality of that experience is hard to measure, and almost impossible to quantify. This is why you will likely have people who are purely numbers-driven not understanding why something is being added to a customer's experience for "no immediate financial gain." But in the long term, there definitely is.

I started the book by mentioning in the introduction my purpose, to bring more Mickey Boat Moments to those around me. Specifically, more of those moments to me, my family and loved ones, and the good people I surround myself with.

One of the reasons my son was so excited about our holiday was the little touches Disney has. On board their ships, if you ask for ketchup, the waiter comes over and adds it to your plate in the famous Mickey Mouse silhouette. That isn't something that is quantifiable in the grand scheme of things, but those little touches are the reason they can command such a higher fee than other cruises with the same itinerary, and often bigger ships.

That sometimes confuses those who are solely driven by numbers. And for clarity, that could still be you. You could be solely driven by numbers, and that is fine. However, if you don't have the understanding and learnings in this book around how those smaller points in a customer journey combine to fill that bottom line, it can have an overall negative impact.

Once you start taking those small things out of the quality of the customer experience, things start to go downhill. The real killer to a business in that scenario is that often there aren't big impacts that are obvious.

In the UK, when you order a Chinese takeaway, typically you will always get a bag of prawn crackers. It's an unwritten rule essentially. The numbers person in a business will say you can remove that because they aren't paying for it. And if they did, they might get a couple of complaints, but the numbers person will say, "We only had a couple of complaints, overall it has worked and we are saving £xx." But over the coming months, your regular customers will start to disappear, and choose someone else, and you will never know that has happened.

The seemingly small things in your customer journey matter, and I hope that by now you have seen focusing on the quality of that journey from the perspective that they really don't give a shit about you, can actually transform how they interact and get them to turn into someone who starts caring.

By implementing the learnings in this book, those prospects who really don't give a shit will turn into regular customers, repeat recommenders and referral machines.

The biggest thing you should take away from this book is that everything should be viewed through the eyes of taking someone who doesn't give a shit, to someone who gives you money. Get that right, and everyone who does care will glide through the process. Get that right, and your business will be able to scale, grow and help more people. Get that right, and you can sit back knowing that everyone is going through a consistent process.

Alongside this book, I've created a library of online resources and example customer journeys that can help you plan out your own experience for your business and will help inspire changes you put into practice. You will also find recordings from previous talks, presentations and trainings that have been done. Scan the QR code below to access those trainings completely free.

Applications to work together are also open, provided we believe we can help and we are a values match. For information on how that works, send me the word **APPLY** on WhatsApp after scanning the code above.

Finally, remember your customers are the people who keep your business alive. They are the ones who give you money, who pay your bills and who decide whether you succeed or fail. Their experience with you dictates that, so make sure it is a good one.

References

[1] Barton, Darren. Business population estimates for the UK and regions 2022: statistical release, https://www.gov.uk/government/statistics/business-population-estimates-2022/business-population-estimates-for-the-uk-and-regions-2022-statistical-release-html#headline-statistics

[2] Modern Wisdom with Chris Williamson Podcast, "Surprising Insights Into Human Psychology, https://youtu.be/DaYTvwe0Wo0?si=otK3dnKm4xQzzS5H

[3] "Fascinating Facts You Never Learned in School", https://www.wd40.com/history/

[4] Barber, Sophie and Boyle, Matthew. "Digital Wallet Statistics: Usage and Market Size", https://www.finder.com/uk/banking/digital-wallet-statistics, May 3, 2024.

[5] Clay, Robert. "Why you must follow up leads," https://www.marketingdonut.co.uk/sales/sales-strategy/why-you-must-follow-up-leads

Printed in Great Britain
by Amazon

57524318R10155